FROM THE KITCHENS OF

HEALTHY CHOICE

FOODS

STIR-FRY
Etc.

MEALS FOR LIFE™

CY DeCOSSE

INCORPORATED

A COWLES MAGAZINES COMPANY

CY DECOSSE INCORPORATED
A COWLES MAGAZINES COMPANY

Chairman/CEO: Bruce Barnet
Chairman Emeritus: Cy DeCosse
President/COO: Nino Tarantino
Executive V.P./Editor-in-Chief:
  William B. Jones

Healthy Choice© is a registered trademark of ConAgra Inc.
used under license by Cy DeCosse Incorporated.

Printed on American paper by:
Quebecor Graphics (0196)
Copyright © 1996
Cy DeCosse Incorporated
5900 Green Oak Drive
Minnetonka, Minnesota 55343
1-800-328-3895
All rights reserved
Printed in U.S.A.

Library of Congress Cataloging-in-Publication Data

Stir-fry etc.
   p. cm. -- (Meals for life™)
   Includes index.
   ISBN 0-86573-977-3
   1. Stir frying.   2. Wok cookery.   3. Skillet cookery.
    I. Cy DeCosse Incorporated. II. Series.
TX689.5.S743   1996
641.7'7--dc20   95-41576

Table of Contents

Stir-fry Etc. shows you a variety of ways to prepare recipes on the stovetop. Cooking in a skillet or wok is a fast and easy way to prepare your main dish, eliminates the need to heat up the oven and allows you to prepare side dishes at the last minute if your main dish takes more effort and time.

The *Etc.* in the title takes the recipes in this book beyond the traditional Oriental stir-fry, although many recipes of that type are included. Skillets and woks are used to stir-fry, sauté and braise. Both main-dish and side-dish recipes use these techniques, so you'll find additional recipes in this book that use other cooking techniques to comp ment skillet and wok recipes not only flavorwis but with ease of preparation in mind.

Menu suggestions appear with every recipe to aid in meal planning. These suggestions includ recipes from this book as well as simple compl mentary dishes.

Menu suggestions focus only on the main comp nents of the meal. Beverages and dessert ideas are not included. Balance the menus with fresh fruit and vegetables, low-fat milk, and breads. Choose low-fat, refreshing desserts like fruit, s bet or angel food cake.

Equipment

The equipment needed for stir-frying, sautéing and braising is minimal. Nonstick skillets and heavy-duty woks are especially helpful in keeping fat use to a minimum. Nylon or wooden utensils allow you to stir food vigorously without scratching the pans. Lids prevent spattering and allow foods like chicken pieces to braise or simmer briefly for thorough cooking.

(1) 6-inch or 8-inch nonstick skillet; **(2)** 12-inch nonstick skillet; **(3)** lid for skillet; **(4)** wooden and **(5)** nylon cooking utensils; **(6)** wok; **(7)** lid for wok

ir-frying & Sautéing

ir-frying is a cooking technique in which small, iform-size pieces of meat and/or vegetables are oked quickly over high heat while being constantly stirred. Sauté literally means "to jump" and defined as cooking food in a small amount of fat while stirring and tossing it. The biggest difference between the two techniques is that food is usually cooked at a slightly lower heat when sautéing, so it doesn't require constant stirring.

Cooking over high heat goes fast, so if several ingredients need to be added to the skillet or wok in rapid succession, have each ingredient cut up and ready in dishes next to the stove.

To stir-fry or sauté, heat a small amount of oil, butter or margarine in a skillet or wok over medium to high heat. Add the ingredients, and stir frequently or constantly to cook evenly and prevent sticking or burning. Add liquids with thickeners, such as a cornstarch mixture, at the end of cooking, since they thicken very quickly.

Braising

Braising meats and vegetables means to brown them first in a small amount of fat, then reduce the heat, cover the skillet and simmer the food in a small amount of liquid until done. This technique allows larger pieces of food to cook thoroughly and blends flavors. Braising also gives you a little extra time to prepare other parts of the meal.

7

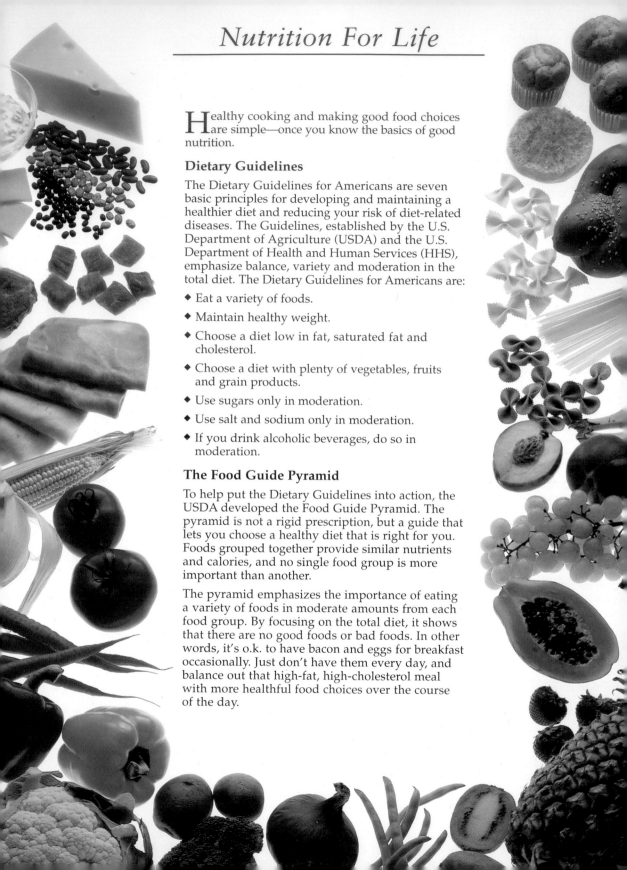

Nutrition For Life

Healthy cooking and making good food choices are simple—once you know the basics of good nutrition.

Dietary Guidelines

The Dietary Guidelines for Americans are seven basic principles for developing and maintaining a healthier diet and reducing your risk of diet-related diseases. The Guidelines, established by the U.S. Department of Agriculture (USDA) and the U.S. Department of Health and Human Services (HHS), emphasize balance, variety and moderation in the total diet. The Dietary Guidelines for Americans are:

- ◆ Eat a variety of foods.
- ◆ Maintain healthy weight.
- ◆ Choose a diet low in fat, saturated fat and cholesterol.
- ◆ Choose a diet with plenty of vegetables, fruits and grain products.
- ◆ Use sugars only in moderation.
- ◆ Use salt and sodium only in moderation.
- ◆ If you drink alcoholic beverages, do so in moderation.

The Food Guide Pyramid

To help put the Dietary Guidelines into action, the USDA developed the Food Guide Pyramid. The pyramid is not a rigid prescription, but a guide that lets you choose a healthy diet that is right for you. Foods grouped together provide similar nutrients and calories, and no single food group is more important than another.

The pyramid emphasizes the importance of eating a variety of foods in moderate amounts from each food group. By focusing on the total diet, it shows that there are no good foods or bad foods. In other words, it's o.k. to have bacon and eggs for breakfast occasionally. Just don't have them every day, and balance out that high-fat, high-cholesterol meal with more healthful food choices over the course of the day.

The Food Guide Pyramid

Fats, Oils & Sweets
Use sparingly

**Milk, Yogurt &
Cheese Group**
2-3 Servings per day

**Meat, Poultry, Fish, Dry
Beans, Eggs & Nuts Group**
2-3 Servings per day

Vegetable Group
3-5 Servings per day

Fruit Group
2-4 Servings per day

**Bread, Cereal, Rice
& Pasta Group**
6-11 Servings
per day

Reading the Pyramid

It's easy to follow the Food Guide Pyramid.

The bottom of the pyramid shows complex carbohydrates—the bread, cereal, rice and pasta group—at 6-11 servings a day. This group should be the foundation of a healthy diet.

The second level is made up of fruits and vegetables. We need to eat 3-5 servings of vegetables and 2-4 servings of fruit each day.

The third level is divided equally between milk, yogurt and cheese (2-3 servings a day) and meat, poultry, fish, beans, eggs and nuts (2-3 servings a day).

Most supermarkets now carry skim or low-fat milk and buttermilk; low-fat or nonfat yogurt, cottage cheese or ricotta cheese; and other low-fat cheeses.

A large variety of lean cuts of meat is also available in most stores. The leanest cuts of beef are the round, loin, sirloin and chuck arm. Pork tenderloin, center loin or lean ham, and all cuts of veal, except ground veal, are relatively lean. For lamb, the leanest cuts are the leg, loin and foreshanks. Chicken and turkey with the skin removed and most fish are lean meat choices.

The tip of the pyramid shows fats, oils and sweets. These include foods such as salad dressings, cream, butter, margarine, sugars, soft drinks and candies. Use them sparingly.

Build a diet of good food choices based on complex carbohydrates, and limit your intake of high-fat foods. The recipes in this book make it easy to fit nutritious meals into a busy schedule. And you don't have to choose between good taste and good nutrition. You can have them both.

Balancing Your Diet

The number of servings per day that is right for you depends on the amount of calories you need to maintain your best weight. The USDA recommends the following calorie levels per day: 1600 calories for many sedentary women and some older adults; 2200 calories for most children, teenage girls, active women and many sedentary men; and 2800 calories for teenage boys, many active men and some very active women. Each person's body is different, however, and you may need more or less depending on your age, sex, size, activity level and medical condition.

For example, if your calorie intake level is in the lower range, choose the smaller number of servings in each food group. Or, if you are very active, choose the larger number of servings in each group.

Serving Sizes

What counts as a serving?

You may be surprised. Use this chart to determine how your food intake compares to servings on the pyramid.

For combination foods, use your best judgment in estimating which food groups they fall into. For example, a large serving of pasta with tomato sauce and cheese could count in the bread group, the vegetable group and the milk group.

Milk, Yogurt & Cheese Group

2 ounces processed cheese, preferably reduced fat

1 cup low-fat milk or yogurt

1½ ounces natural cheese, preferably reduced fat

Meat, Poultry & Fish Group

½ cup cooked dry beans, 1 egg or 2 tablespoons peanut butter count as 1 ounce lean meat

2-3 ounces cooked lean meat, poultry or fish

Vegetable Group

1 cup raw leafy vegetables

½ cup other vegetables, cooked or raw

¾ cup vegetable juice

Fruit Group

¾ cup fruit juice

½ cup chopped, cooked or canned fruit

1 medium apple, banana or orange

Bread, Cereal, Rice & Pasta Group

1 muffin, dinner roll or slice bread

1 ounce ready-to-eat cereal

½ cup cooked cereal, rice or pasta

2 Add juice, wine, sugar, salt, marjoram and pepper to skillet. Cover. Reduce heat to low. Let simmer for 12 to 15 minutes, or until meat near bone is no longer pink and juices run clear.

3 Remove chicken from skillet and place on serving platter. Cover to keep warm. Set aside. Using whisk, stir cornstarch mixture into skillet. Add grapes and peel. Cook for 1½ to 2½ minutes, or until sauce is thickened and translucent, stirring constantly. Spoon over chicken.

Nutrition Facts	Amount/serving	%DV*	Amount/serving	%DV*
Serving Size 1 breast half (136g) Servings per Recipe 6 Calories 164 Calories from Fat 41	Total Fat 5g	7%	Total Carbohydrate 9g	3%
	Saturated Fat 1g	5%	Dietary Fiber <1g	1%
	Cholesterol 55mg	18%	Sugars 8g	
	Sodium 135mg	6%	Protein 21g	
	Vitamin A 0% • Vitamin C 20% • Calcium 2% • Iron 4% *Percent Daily Values (DV) are based on a 2000 calorie diet.			

Menu Planning Guide
One serving of this recipe provides:
1 Meat, Poultry & Fish
½ Fruit

Diet Exchanges:
3 lean meat • ½ fruit

Nutritional Information

Each recipe in this book is followed by a Nutrition Facts chart and diet exchanges. The Nutrition Facts chart is similar to those that appear on food product labels. The diet exchange system is used by people with diabetes and persons on a weight-control diet, to estimate the calories, protein, carbohydrate and fat content of a food or meal. Diet exchanges are based on exchange lists and are not the same as pyramid servings.

Nutrition Facts state serving size, servings per container and the amount of calories, calories from fat and other nutrients per serving. Percentage of Daily Value gives you an idea of what percentage of the day's nutrients comes from the recipe. The percentages of the Daily Value of fat, saturated fat, cholesterol, sodium, total carbohydrate and dietary fiber are based on a 2,000-calorie-per-day diet. (Daily values will vary from person to person depending on calorie needs.) The Dietary Guidelines recommend that no more than 30% of your calories come from fat. So, if you are eating 2,000 calories per day, your total fat intake should be less than 65 grams.

If alternate ingredients are given in the recipe's ingredient list, such as a choice between cholesterol-free egg product and egg, the nutritional analysis applies to the first ingredient listed. Optional ingredients are not included in the analysis. For pasta and rice, the nutritional information applies to the plain, boiled item without salt or fat added.

Recipe serving sizes are based on federal reference numbers for serving sizes.

The Pyramid in This Book

Each recipe in this book includes a Menu Planning Guide that shows the number of servings from each pyramid group that one serving of that recipe provides. A daily total of these "pyramid servings" shows how your diet compares to the USDA recommendations.

When the tip of the pyramid has a dot, the item may contain added fat or fat beyond the natural fat content of lean or low-fat items in the food groups. Refer to the Nutrition Facts chart to check the total amount of fat per serving. A tip with a dot may also indicate that the recipe contains added sugar. Refer to the recipe to determine the number of teaspoons of sugar you will eat.

The number of servings is rounded to the nearest half. If no figures appear next to or within the pyramid, it means that serving sizes are negligible.

If the tip of the pyramid has no dot, a serving contains less than 3 grams added fat or less than 1 teaspoon added sugar.

Szechuan Barbecue Pork & Vegetables

Serve with hot cooked white rice and mandarin orange segments

½ cup light barbecue sauce

2 to 3 tablespoons honey

2 tablespoons reduced-sodium soy sauce

¼ to ½ teaspoon crushed red pepper flakes

12-oz. pork tenderloin, sliced (½-inch slices)

1 pkg. (10 oz.) frozen whole baby carrots

4 oz. fresh snow pea pods (1½ cups)

4 servings

1 Combine barbecue sauce, honey, soy sauce and red pepper flakes in 2-cup measure. Set aside. Spray 12-inch nonstick skillet or wok skillet with nonstick vegetable cooking spray. Heat skillet over medium heat. Add pork slices. Cook for 4 to 6 minutes, or just until no longer pink, stirring occasionally.

2 Add sauce mixture and carrots. Cook for 10 minutes. Add pea pods. Cook for 5 to 8 minutes, or until pea pods are bright green and mixture is hot, stirring occasionally.

Nutrition Facts	Amount/serving	%DV*	Amount/serving	%DV*
Serving Size approximately 1 cup	Total Fat 3g	5%	Total Carbohydrate 24g	8%
Servings per Recipe 4	Saturated Fat 1g	6%	Dietary Fiber 3g	13%
Calories 214	Cholesterol 53mg	18%	Sugars 13g	
Calories from Fat 30	Sodium 613mg	26%	Protein 21g	

Vitamin A 130% • Vitamin C 35% • Calcium 4% • Iron 15%

*Percent Daily Values (DV) are based on a 2000 calorie diet.

Menu Planning Guide

One serving of this recipe provides:

1 Meat, Poultry & Fish
1 Vegetable

Diet Exchanges:

2 lean meat • 1 starch • 1 vegetable

Beef Stroganoff

*Serve with Sweet-spiced Brussels Sprouts & Apples (p 85)
or Braised Celery Root (p 64)*

 4   cups uncooked mini lasagna noodles
 1/3 cup dry white wine or ready-to-serve
     beef broth
 1/3 cup spicy vegetable juice
 1/4 cup water
 2   tablespoons all-purpose flour
 1/4 teaspoon salt
 1/4 teaspoon pepper
 1 - lb. boneless beef sirloin steak, 1 1/2 inches
     thick, cut into 2 1/2 x 1/4-inch strips
 6   oz. fresh mushrooms, quartered (2 cups)
 1   medium onion, chopped (1 cup)
 1/3 cup nonfat or low-fat sour cream
     Snipped fresh parsley

6 servings

1 Prepare noodles as directed on package. Rinse. Let stand in warm water. In 2-cup measure, combine wine, juice, water, flour, salt and pepper. Set aside.

2 Combine steak, mushrooms and onion in 12-inch nonstick skillet. Cook over medium heat for 8 1/2 to 10 minutes, or until meat is no longer pink, stirring frequently. Add wine mixture to skillet. Cook for 2 1/2 to 5 minutes, or until sauce thickens, stirring constantly. Remove from heat. Stir in sour cream.

3 Drain noodles. Serve stroganoff over noodles. Garnish with snipped fresh parsley.

Hearty Beef Skillet Meal

*Serve with Orange-gingered Acorn Squash (p 76)
or a crisp green salad*

1 pkg. (6¾ oz.) quick-cooking long-grain
   white and wild rice mix

1 can (14½ oz.) ready-to-serve beef broth

¼ cup all-purpose flour

½ teaspoon salt

¼ teaspoon pepper

1 lb. lean ground beef, crumbled

2 medium carrots, chopped (1 cup)

1 medium onion, chopped (1 cup)

1 cup sliced fresh mushrooms

1 stalk celery, sliced (½ cup)

1 teaspoon dried thyme leaves

1 teaspoon dried basil leaves

1 teaspoon dried oregano leaves

½ teaspoon dried marjoram leaves

2 tablespoons snipped fresh parsley

6 servings

1 Prepare rice as directed on package, except discard seasoning packet and omit margarine and salt. Remove from heat. Cover to keep warm. Set aside.

2 Meanwhile, combine broth, flour, salt and pepper in 2-cup measure. Set aside. In 12-inch nonstick skillet, combine beef, carrots, onion, mushrooms, celery, thyme, basil, oregano, and marjoram. Cook over medium heat for 13 to 15 minutes, or until meat is no longer pink and vegetables are tender-crisp, stirring occasionally. Drain.

3 Add broth mixture to skillet. Cook over medium heat for 2 to 3 minutes, or until mixture thickens and bubbles, stirring constantly. Stir in rice. Cook for 1 to 2 minutes, or until heated through, stirring frequently. Remove from heat. Stir in parsley.

Nutrition Facts	Amount/serving	%DV*	Amount/serving	%DV*
Serving Size approximately 1 cup (315g)	Total Fat 10g	16%	Total Carbohydrate 35g	12%
	Saturated Fat 4g	20%	Dietary Fiber 3g	11%
Servings per Recipe 6	Cholesterol 56mg	19%	Sugars 4g	
Calories 326 Calories from Fat 94	Sodium 481mg	20%	Protein 23g	
	Vitamin A 120% • Vitamin C 10% • Calcium 6% • Iron 25%			
	*Percent Daily Values (DV) are based on a 2000 calorie diet.			

Menu Planning Guide

One serving of this recipe provides:

1 Meat, Poultry & Fish
1 Vegetable
1 Bread, Cereal, Rice & Pasta

Diet Exchanges:

2 medium-fat meat • 2 starch • 1 vegetable

Hickory Beef Fajitas

erve with Spanish Rice (p 106) or Rice with Beans & Jalapeños (p 104)

alsa:

1 *medium tomato, chopped (1 cup), divided*
1 *small onion, finely chopped (½ cup)*
1 *jalapeño pepper, seeded and finely chopped*
1 *tablespoon snipped fresh cilantro*

Marinade:

/4 *cup fresh lime juice*
2 *tablespoons to ¼ cup hickory-flavored*
      liquid smoke
2 *tablespoons water*

1 *-lb. well-trimmed beef top sirloin steak,*
      1 inch thick, cut into 3 x ¼-inch strips
4 *flour tortillas (8-inch)*
1 *cup red and green pepper strips*
      (2 x ¼-inch strips)
1 *small onion, cut into 8 wedges*
/4 *cup nonfat or low-fat sour cream*

servings

1 Place ½ cup tomato in food processor or blender. Process until smooth. In small mixing bowl, combine processed tomato, remaining ½ cup tomato and remaining salsa ingredients. Cover with plastic wrap. Chill. In 1-cup measure, combine marinade ingredients. Place steak in shallow dish. Pour marinade over steak, stirring to coat. Cover dish with plastic wrap. Chill 1 hour, stirring occasionally.

2 Heat oven to 325°F. Wrap tortillas in foil. Bake for 7 to 8 minutes, or until tortillas are warm. Set aside, leaving tortillas wrapped in foil to keep warm.

3 Drain and discard marinade from steak. Heat 12-inch nonstick skillet over medium-high heat. Add steak, pepper strips and onion. Cook for 3½ to 5 minutes, or until meat is no longer pink and vegetables are tender-crisp, stirring frequently. Drain.

4 Spoon about 1 cup steak mixture down center of each tortilla. Roll up. Top each fajita with about ¼ cup salsa and 1 table-spoon sour cream.

Nutrition Facts	Amount/serving	%DV*	Amount/serving	%DV*
Serving Size 1 fajita (227g)	Total Fat 10g	15%	Total Carbohydrate 27g	9%
Servings per Recipe 4	Saturated Fat 3g	16%	Dietary Fiber 3g	10%
Calories 329	Cholesterol 80mg	27%	Sugars 4g	
Calories from Fat 90	Sodium 243mg	10%	Protein 32g	

Vitamin A 25% • Vitamin C 90% • Calcium 6% • Iron 25%
*Percent Daily Values (DV) are based on a 2000 calorie diet.

Menu Planning Guide

One serving of this recipe provides:
1 Meat, Poultry & Fish
1 Vegetable
1 Bread, Cereal, Rice & Pasta

Diet Exchanges:

3 lean meat • 1½ starch • 1 vegetable

Hot & Spicy Pork Salad

Serve with a crusty roll or Baked Eggrolls (p 63)

2 tablespoons reduced-sodium soy sauce

1 tablespoon Chinese hot chili sauce with garlic

1-lb. well-trimmed pork tenderloin, cut into
    2 x ¼-inch strips

3 cups shredded leaf and Bibb lettuce

1 cup shredded green cabbage

½ cup shredded carrot

½ cup thinly sliced red pepper
    Unsalted peanuts (optional)

4 servings

1 Combine soy sauce and chili sauce in 1-cup measure. In small mixing bowl, combine pork strips and 1 tablespoon soy sauce mixture. Cover with plastic wrap. Chill 30 minutes.

2 Combine lettuce, cabbage, carrot and pepper in large mixing bowl or salad bowl. Toss to combine. Set aside.

3 Spray 10-inch nonstick skillet with non-stick vegetable cooking spray. Add por Cook over medium heat for 5 to 7 minutes or just until meat is no longer pink, stirrin occasionally. Drain. Add meat and remaining reserved soy sauce mixture to lettuce mixture. Toss to coat. Sprinkle with peanut

Nutrition Facts	Amount/serving	%DV*	Amount/serving	%DV*
Serving Size 1½ cups (188g)	Total Fat 5g	7%	Total Carbohydrate 6g	2%
Servings per Recipe 4	Saturated Fat 2g	8%	Dietary Fiber 2g	8%
Calories 177	Cholesterol 71mg	24%	Sugars 3g	
Calories from Fat 41	Sodium 469mg	20%	Protein 27g	

Vitamin A 110% • Vitamin C 60% • Calcium 4% • Iron 15%
*Percent Daily Values (DV) are based on a 2000 calorie diet.

Menu Planning Guide

One serving of this recipe provides:
1 Meat, Poultry & Fish
1 Vegetable

Diet Exchanges:

3 lean meat • 1 vegetable

Peppercorn Pork Tenderloin

Serve with Veggie-stuffed Zucchini (p 88)
or Cool Tarragon Cucumbers (p 69)

1 -lb. well-trimmed pork tenderloin, cut
    crosswise into ¼-inch slices

1 cup ready-to-serve chicken broth

/4 cup dry white wine

1 tablespoon cornstarch mixed with
    1 tablespoon water

2 to 3 teaspoons coarsely crushed dried green
    peppercorns

2 cloves garlic, minced

1 teaspoon dry mustard

2 cups hot cooked fettucini

servings

1 Spray 10-inch nonstick skillet with non-stick vegetable cooking spray. Heat skillet over medium-high heat. Add pork. Cook for 10 to 12 minutes, or until meat is golden brown on both sides, stirring frequently. Remove pork from skillet. Cover to keep warm. Set aside.

2 Combine remaining ingredients, except fettucini, in same skillet. Cook over medium heat for 3 to 4½ minutes, or until sauce is thickened and translucent, stirring constantly. Add pork. Cook for additional 1 to 2 minutes, or until hot, stirring constantly. Serve pork mixture over fettucini.

Nutrition Facts	Amount/serving	%DV*	Amount/serving	%DV*
Serving Size approximately 1 cup (243g)	Total Fat 5g	8%	Total Carbohydrate 23g	8%
	Saturated Fat 2g	9%	Dietary Fiber 1g	5%
Servings per Recipe 4	Cholesterol 71mg	24%	Sugars 1g	
Calories 268	Sodium 247mg	10%	Protein 30g	
Calories from Fat 48	Vitamin A 0% • Vitamin C 2% • Calcium 2% • Iron 15%			
	*Percent Daily Values (DV) are based on a 2000 calorie diet.			

Menu Planning Guide
One serving of this recipe provides:
1 Meat, Poultry & Fish
1 Bread, Cereal, Rice & Pasta

Diet Exchanges:
3 lean meat • 1½ starch

Plum-sauced Pork Medallions

Serve with hot cooked egg noodles with poppy seed and steamed zucchini slices

¼ cup chopped onion

½ teaspoon vegetable oil

½ cup red plum jam

1 tablespoon red wine vinegar

1 teaspoon reduced-sodium soy sauce

¼ teaspoon ground ginger

2 small plums, each cut into 8 wedges

1 well-trimmed pork tenderloin (approx. 1 lb.), cut crosswise into 8 pieces

Cayenne

servings

1 Spray 8-inch nonstick skillet with non-stick vegetable cooking spray. Add onion and oil. Cook over medium heat for 4 to 7 minutes, or until onion is tender, stirring occasionally. Reduce heat to low. Stir in jam, vinegar, soy sauce and ginger. Cook for 1 to 2 minutes, or until jam is melted, stirring occasionally. Stir in plums. Set sauce aside.

2 Pound pork pieces lightly to 1-inch thickness. Sprinkle both sides of each piece lightly with cayenne. Spray 10-inch nonstick skillet with nonstick vegetable cooking spray. Heat skillet over medium-high heat. Add pork. Cook for 6 to 8 minutes, or just until meat is no longer pink, turning over once. Serve topped with plum sauce.

Microwave tip: Omit oil. Place onion in 2-cup measure. Cover with plastic wrap. Microwave at High for 2 to 3 minutes, or until tender, stirring once. Stir in jam, vinegar, soy sauce and ginger. Microwave at High, uncovered, for 1½ to 2 minutes, or until jam is melted, stirring once. Stir in plums. Set sauce aside. Continue as directed.

Nutrition Facts	Amount/serving	%DV*	Amount/serving	%DV*
Serving Size 2 medallions w/sauce (156g)	Total Fat 5g	8%	Total Carbohydrate 31g	10%
	Saturated Fat 2g	8%	Dietary Fiber 1g	4%
Servings per Recipe 4	Cholesterol 70mg	23%	Sugars 30g	
Calories 272 Calories from Fat 45	Sodium 108mg	5%	Protein 26g	
	Vitamin A 2% • Vitamin C 4% • Calcium 2% • Iron 10%			
	*Percent Daily Values (DV) are based on a 2000 calorie diet.			

Menu Planning Guide

One serving of this recipe provides:

1 Meat, Poultry & Fish

Diet Exchanges:

3 lean meat • 2 fruit

Ragout of Lamb

Serve with hot cooked couscous and Spicy Moroccan Vegetables (p 78)

1 - lb. well-trimmed boneless lamb leg roast,
   cut into ¾-inch pieces

1 can (14½ oz.) diced tomatoes

2 medium carrots, cut into 1½ x ¼-inch
   strips (1½ cups)

2 teaspoons chili powder

¼ to ½ teaspoon ground cinnamon

½ teaspoon sugar

¼ teaspoon salt

1 cup green pepper chunks (½-inch chunks)

4 servings

Note: Ragout is a thick, well-seasoned stew of
meat, poultry or fish, made with or without
vegetables. It is from a French word meaning
"to stimulate the appetite."

1 Spray 12-inch nonstick skillet with non-stick vegetable cooking spray. Add lamb. Cook over medium heat for 4 to 6 minutes, or just until meat is only slightly pink, stirring occasionally. Drain.

2 Stir in remaining ingredients, except pepper chunks. Cover. Cook over medium heat for 10 minutes, stirring occasionally. Stir in pepper chunks. Re-cover. Cook over medium heat for 7 to 9 minutes, or until vegetables are tender, stirring occasionally.

Nutrition Facts	Amount/serving	%DV*	Amount/serving	%DV*
Serving Size 1 cup (238g)	Total Fat 6g	10%	Total Carbohydrate 11g	4%
Servings per Recipe 4	Saturated Fat 2g	10%	Dietary Fiber 3g	12%
Calories 188	Cholesterol 64mg	21%	Sugars 6g	
Calories from Fat 56	Sodium 376mg	16%	Protein 22g	

Vitamin A 230% • Vitamin C 70% • Calcium 6% • Iron 15%

*Percent Daily Values (DV) are based on a 2000 calorie diet.

Menu Planning Guide
One serving of this recipe provides:
1 Meat, Poultry & Fish
2 Vegetable

Diet Exchanges:
2½ lean meat • 2 vegetable

Spicy Beef with Peppers & Oranges

Serve with hot cooked curly noodles and steamed snow pea pods or broccoli

1 - lb. well-trimmed beef top sirloin steak, 1 inch
   thick, cut into 2 x ⅛-inch strips

1 medium seedless orange

1 tablespoon reduced-sodium soy sauce

½ teaspoon ground ginger

½ teaspoon cayenne

⅛ teaspoon garlic powder

1½ teaspoons cornstarch

½ cup water

2 cups red or green pepper chunks
   (¾-inch chunks)

4 servings

1 Place beef strips in medium mixing bowl. Set aside. Grate 1½ teaspoons peel from orange. Set aside. Remove and discard remaining peel. Cut orange into ¼-inch slices. Cut each slice in half. Set aside. Sprinkle meat with 1 teaspoon reserved peel, the soy sauce, ginger, cayenne and garlic powder. Toss to coat.

2 Spray 12-inch nonstick skillet with nonstick vegetable cooking spray. Heat skillet over medium heat. Add meat mixture. Cook for 2 to 3 minutes, or until meat is only slightly pink, stirring frequently. Using slotted spoon, remove meat from skillet. Set aside.

3 Wipe skillet with paper towel. In same skillet, combine cornstarch and remaining ½ teaspoon peel. Blend in water. Add pepper chunks. Cook over medium heat for 3 to 5 minutes, or until mixture is thickened and translucent and peppers are tender-crisp, stirring frequently. Stir in meat and orange pieces. Cook 1½ to 2 minutes, or until hot, stirring occasionally.

Nutrition Facts

Serving Size approximately 1 cup (226g)
Servings per Recipe 4
Calories 216
Calories from Fat 60

Amount/serving	%DV*	Amount/serving	%DV*
Total Fat 7g	10%	Total Carbohydrate 10g	3%
Saturated Fat 3g	13%	Dietary Fiber 2g	8%
Cholesterol 80mg	27%	Sugars 5g	
Sodium 211mg	9%	Protein 28g	

Vitamin A 70% • Vitamin C 210% • Calcium 4% • Iron 20%
*Percent Daily Values (DV) are based on a 2000 calorie diet.

Menu Planning Guide

One serving of this recipe provides:
1 Meat, Poultry & Fish
1 Vegetable

Diet Exchanges:

3 lean meat • 1 vegetable

Spicy Spaghetti with Beef & Vegetables

Serve with a whole wheat role and tossed salad or Caponata (p 66)

1 pkg. (7 oz.) uncooked spaghetti

/2 lb. lean ground beef, crumbled

/4 cup chopped onion

1 can (15 oz.) tomato sauce

1 tablespoon red wine vinegar

1 teaspoon Italian seasoning

/2 teaspoon sugar

/4 teaspoon garlic powder

/4 teaspoon crushed red pepper flakes

1 medium zucchini, thinly sliced (1 cup)

1 medium tomato, seeded and coarsely
   chopped (1 cup)

2 tablespoons to 1/4 cup snipped fresh parsley

servings

1 Prepare spaghetti as directed on package. Rinse with hot water. Drain. Set aside.

2 Combine beef and onion in 10-inch non-stick skillet. Cook over medium heat for 4 to 5 minutes, or until meat is no longer pink, stirring occasionally. Stir in tomato sauce, vinegar, Italian seasoning, sugar, garlic powder and red pepper flakes. Cook over medium heat for 2 to 4 minutes, or until hot and bubbly, stirring occasionally.

3 Stir in prepared spaghetti and zucchini. Cook for 2 to 3 minutes, or until hot, stirring occasionally. Stir in tomato and parsley. Serve hot.

Nutrition Facts	Amount/serving	%DV*	Amount/serving	%DV*
Serving Size approximately 1 cup (251g)	Total Fat 2g	3%	Total Carbohydrate 34g	11%
Servings per Recipe 6	Saturated Fat <1g	2%	Dietary Fiber 3g	12%
Calories 196	Cholesterol 15mg	5%	Sugars 6g	
Calories from Fat 17	Sodium 503mg	21%	Protein 11g	

Vitamin A 20% • Vitamin C 30% • Calcium 2% • Iron 15%
*Percent Daily Values (DV) are based on a 2000 calorie diet.

Menu Planning Guide

One serving of this recipe provides:
- 1/2 Meat, Poultry & Fish
- 1 1/2 Vegetable
- 1 1/2 Bread, Cereal, Rice & Pasta

Diet Exchanges:

1 lean meat • 1 1/2 starch • 1 1/2 vegetable

Beef Bourguignonne

Serve with Summer Squash Scramble (p 82)
or Green Bean Sauté (p 70)

¼ cup burgundy or other dry red wine, divided

½ cup ready-to-serve beef broth

½ cup water

1 teaspoon paprika

1 bay leaf

½ teaspoon caraway seed

¼ teaspoon celery seed

1 - lb. well-trimmed boneless chuck roast,
    ¾ inch thick

⅓ cup finely chopped shallots

1 cup sliced fresh mushrooms

1 teaspoon all-purpose flour mixed with
    2 teaspoons water

servings

1 Combine ½ cup wine, the broth, water, paprika, bay leaf, caraway seed and celery seed in 2-cup measure. Set aside.

2 Heat 6-quart Dutch oven or 12-inch nonstick skillet over medium-high heat. Add roast and shallots. Cook for 6 to 7 minutes, or until meat is browned on both sides. Drain.

3 Pour wine mixture over roast. Bring to boil. Cover. Reduce heat to low. Simmer for 1½ to 2 hours, or until meat is very tender. Transfer roast to serving platter. Cover to keep warm. Set aside.

4 Stir remaining ¼ cup wine and the mushrooms into pan drippings. Cook over medium heat for 3 to 5 minutes, or just until mushrooms are tender, stirring occasionally. Stir in flour mixture. Cook for 1 to 2 minutes, or until sauce is thickened and slightly reduced, stirring constantly. Serve sauce with roast.

Nutrition Facts	Amount/serving	%DV*	Amount/serving	%DV*
Serving Size ¼ roast with sauce (223g)	Total Fat 5g	8%	Total Carbohydrate 5g	2%
	Saturated Fat 2g	9%	Dietary Fiber 1g	4%
Servings per Recipe 4	Cholesterol 73mg	24%	Sugars 1g	
Calories 171	Sodium 153mg	6%	Protein 26g	
Calories from Fat 45	Vitamin A 40% • Vitamin C 4% • Calcium 2% • Iron 20%			
	*Percent Daily Values (DV) are based on a 2000 calorie diet.			

Menu Planning Guide
One serving of this recipe provides:
  1 Meat, Poultry & Fish
½ Vegetable

Diet Exchanges:
3 lean meat • ½ vegetable

Artichoke Turkey Hash

Serve with Hot Spinach Toss (p 73) and a buttermilk biscuit

1 lb. ground turkey (breast meat only; no skin), crumbled

2 cups frozen shredded hash browns

1 can (14 oz.) artichoke hearts in water, rinsed, drained and coarsely chopped

1 jar (2 oz.) sliced pimiento, drained

2 tablespoons snipped fresh parsley

/2 teaspoon dried thyme leaves

/4 teaspoon salt

/4 teaspoon freshly ground pepper

/8 teaspoon ground nutmeg

servings

1 Combine all ingredients in large mixing bowl. Spray 12-inch nonstick skillet with nonstick vegetable cooking spray. Heat over medium heat. Spread turkey mixture evenly in skillet. Cook for 8 to 13 minutes, or until turkey is no longer pink and hash is golden brown, stirring occasionally.

Menu Planning Guide

One serving of this recipe provides:

1 Meat, Poultry & Fish
2 Vegetable

Diet Exchanges:

2 lean meat • 1 starch • 2 vegetable

Country French Skillet Dinner

Serve with Cool Tarragon Cucumbers (p 69) and French bread

1 teaspoon olive oil

2 boneless whole chicken breasts (8 to 10 oz. each), split in half, skin removed, cut into 1½ x 1-inch pieces

8 oz. fresh mushrooms, quartered (3 cups)

2 cloves garlic, minced

1 cup ready-to-serve chicken broth

1 teaspoon Worcestershire sauce

½ teaspoon dried basil leaves

¼ teaspoon dried marjoram leaves

¼ teaspoon freshly ground pepper

1 lb. small new potatoes, thinly sliced (3 cups)

3 medium carrots, cut into 2 x ¼-inch strips (1½ cups)

½ cup thinly sliced green onions

4 servings

1 Heat oil in 12-inch nonstick skillet over medium-high heat. Add chicken. Cook for 4 to 5 minutes, or just until lightly browned on all sides, stirring frequently.

2 Reduce heat to medium-low. Add mushrooms and garlic. Cook for 4 to 5 minutes, or until mushrooms are lightly browned, stirring frequently.

3 Stir in broth, Worcestershire sauce, basil, marjoram and pepper. Bring mixture to boil over medium-high heat. Add potatoes and carrots. Reduce heat to medium-low. Cover. Simmer for 12 to 15 minutes, or until potatoes are tender. Stir in green onions.

Nutrition Facts	Amount/serving	%DV*	Amount/serving	%DV*
Serving Size approximately 1 cup (406g) Servings per Recipe 4	Total Fat 4g	7%	Total Carbohydrate 36g	12%
	Saturated Fat 1g	5%	Dietary Fiber 6g	24%
	Cholesterol 54mg	18%	Sugars 5g	
Calories 284 Calories from Fat 39	Sodium 295mg	12%	Protein 27g	
	Vitamin A 270% • Vitamin C 35% • Calcium 6% • Iron 15%			
	*Percent Daily Values (DV) are based on a 2000 calorie diet.			

Menu Planning Guide
One serving of this recipe provides:
1 Meat, Poultry & Fish
3 Vegetable

Diet Exchanges:
2½ lean meat • 1½ starch • 2 vegetable

Gingered Turkey Stir-fry

Serve with hot cooked white rice or curly noodles
and Sushi Sandwiches (p 91)

Marinade:

1 egg white, slightly beaten

2 teaspoons cornstarch

2 teaspoons soy sauce

1 teaspoon sugar

1/2 teaspoon white pepper

2 turkey tenderloins (8 to 10 oz. each), cut
　　into 1/8-inch strips

Sauce:

1 cup ready-to-serve chicken broth

1 tablespoon cornstarch

1 tablespoon soy sauce

8 cups water

3 cups coarsely chopped bok choy

3 oz. fresh snow pea pods (1 cup)

1 tablespoon grated fresh gingerroot

1 clove garlic, minced

2 medium carrots, thinly sliced diagonally
　　(1 cup)

1 1/2 oz. fresh shiitake mushrooms, stems
　　removed and thinly sliced (1 cup)

1 small onion, cut in half lengthwise and
　　thinly sliced (1/2 cup)

6 servings

1 Combine marinade ingredients in mediu
mixing bowl. Add turkey strips, stirrin
to coat. Cover with plastic wrap. Chill. In
small mixing bowl, combine sauce ingredi
ents. Set aside.

2 Bring water to boil over high heat in
4-quart saucepan. Immerse bok choy
and pea pods in water for 30 to 40 second
or until color brightens. Remove with slot
ted spoon. Drain well. Set aside.

3 Heat 12-inch nonstick skillet over
medium-high heat. Add turkey mixtur
Cook for 3 to 5 minutes, or until meat is n
longer pink, stirring constantly. Remove
turkey from skillet.

4 Add gingerroot and garlic to same
skillet. Stir in bok choy, pea pods, carrots, mushrooms and onion. Cook for 3 to
minutes, or until onion is tender-crisp,
stirring constantly.

5 Return turkey to skillet. Cook for 1 to 2
minutes, or until hot, stirring constantl
Add sauce. Cook for 1 to 2 minutes, or un
sauce is thickened and translucent, stirrin
constantly.

Nutrition Facts	Amount/serving	%DV*	Amount/serving	%DV*
Serving Size 1 cup (587g)	Total Fat 1g	2%	Total Carbohydrate 14g	5%
Servings per Recipe 6	Saturated Fat <1g	2%	Dietary Fiber 3g	13%
Calories 150	Cholesterol 48mg	16%	Sugars 4g	
Calories from Fat 11	Sodium 510mg	21%	Protein 21g	

Vitamin A 160% • Vitamin C 60% • Calcium 10% • Iron 15%
*Percent Daily Values (DV) are based on a 2000 calorie diet.

Menu Planning Guide

One serving of this recipe provides:
1　Meat, Poultry & Fish
2　Vegetable

Diet Exchanges:

2 lean meat • 2 vegetable

Lemon Chicken & Vegetables

Serve with Basmati & Wild Rice with Fennel (p 92)
or steamed new potatoes

2 *tablespoons unseasoned dry bread crumbs*

2 *boneless whole chicken breasts (8 to 10 oz.*
   each), split in half, skin removed, pounded
   to 1/4-inch thickness

2 *teaspoons olive oil, divided*

1 *small zucchini, cut into 1 1/2 x 1/4-inch*
   strips (1 cup)

1/2 *cup red pepper strips (2 x 1/4-inch strips)*

1/2 *cup thinly sliced red onion*

1 *clove garlic, minced*

2 *tablespoons fresh lemon juice*

1/2 *teaspoon dried rosemary leaves*

1/8 *teaspoon crushed red pepper flakes (optional)*

1 *tablespoon all-purpose flour mixed with*
   3/4 cup ready-to-serve chicken broth

1/2 *teaspoon grated lemon peel (optional)*
   Fresh lemon juice (optional)

servings

1 Place bread crumbs in shallow dish.
Dredge chicken in bread crumbs to coat.
Spray 12-inch nonstick skillet with nonstick
vegetable cooking spray. Add 1 teaspoon
oil. Heat oil over medium heat. Add chick-
en. Cook for 6 to 8 minutes, or just until
meat is no longer pink and juices run clear,
turning chicken over once. Remove chicken
from pan. Cover to keep warm. Set aside.

2 Combine remaining 1 teaspoon oil, the
zucchini, pepper strips, onion and garlic
in same skillet. Cook over medium heat for
3 to 4 minutes, or until vegetables are tender-
crisp, stirring frequently. Stir in 2 tablespoons
juice, the rosemary and red pepper flakes.
Cook for 1 minute, stirring frequently. Stir
in flour mixture. Cook for 1 to 2 minutes,
or until mixture thickens and bubbles, stirring frequently.

3 Return chicken to skillet. Cook for 1
to 2 minutes, or until chicken is hot.
Remove from heat. Serve chicken topped
with vegetables. Garnish with peel and
additional juice.

Nutrition Facts	Amount/serving	%DV*	Amount/serving	%DV*
Serving Size 1/2 breast with vegetables (220g)	Total Fat 5g	8%	Total Carbohydrate 9g	3%
	Saturated Fat 1g	6%	Dietary Fiber 1g	6%
Servings per Recipe 4	Cholesterol 64mg	21%	Sugars 3g	
Calories 193	Sodium 223mg	9%	Protein 26g	
Calories from Fat 49	Vitamin A 20% • Vitamin C 60% • Calcium 4% • Iron 8%			
	*Percent Daily Values (DV) are based on a 2000 calorie diet.			

Menu Planning Guide
One serving of this recipe provides:
1 Meat, Poultry & Fish
1 Vegetable

Diet Exchanges:
3 lean meat • 1 vegetable

Spicy Chicken Wontons

Serve with Chinese-style Fish with Vegetables (p 51),
Vegetable Shrimp Stir-fry (p 60) or Vegetable Fried Rice (p 109)

1/2 lb. ground chicken (breast meat only; no
    skin), crumbled

1/2 cup finely chopped water chestnuts

1/4 cup thinly sliced green onions

1 clove garlic, minced

1/2 teaspoon grated fresh gingerroot

1 tablespoon dry sherry (optional)

1 to 2 teaspoons soy sauce

1/4 to 1/2 teaspoon crushed red pepper flakes

1/8 to 1/4 teaspoon red pepper sauce

30 wonton skins

10 servings

Tip: To prevent wonton skins from drying out,
keep them covered with plastic wrap until ready
to bake.

1 Heat oven to 375°F. Spray baking sheets
with nonstick vegetable cooking spray.
Set aside. In 10-inch nonstick skillet, combine chicken, water chestnuts, onions, garli
and gingerroot. Cook over medium-high
heat for 4 to 5 1/2 minutes, or until meat is
no longer pink, stirring frequently. Drain.
Stir in sherry, soy sauce, pepper flakes and
pepper sauce.

2 Place 1 scant tablespoon chicken mixtur
in center of each wonton skin. Fold one
corner over filling to form triangles. Seal
edges with water. Place triangles on prepared baking sheets. Spray triangle tops
with nonstick vegetable cooking spray.
Bake, one sheet at a time, for 12 to 14 minutes, or until golden brown. Serve with
additional soy sauce, if desired.

Nutrition Facts	Amount/serving	%DV*	Amount/serving	%DV*
Serving Size 3 wontons (60g) Servings per Recipe 10 Calories 135 Calories from Fat 10	Total Fat 1g	2%	Total Carbohydrate 22g	7%
	Saturated Fat 0g	2%	Dietary Fiber 0g	0%
	Cholesterol 17mg	6%	Sugars 0g	
	Sodium 242mg	10%	Protein 9g	
	Vitamin A 0% • Vitamin C 2% • Calcium 2% • Iron 8%			
	*Percent Daily Values (DV) are based on a 2000 calorie diet.			

Menu Planning Guide

One serving of this recipe provides:
  1 Bread, Cereal, Rice & Pasta

Diet Exchanges:

1/2 lean meat • 1 1/2 starch

Spring Lemon Chicken

Serve with Hot Pasta Salad (p 98) or Green Bean Sauté (p 70)

3 bone-in whole chicken breasts
   (10 to 12 oz. each), split in half,
   skin removed

1/8 teaspoon white pepper

1 teaspoon olive oil

1 tablespoon grated lemon peel

2 tablespoons fresh lemon juice

1 tablespoon honey

6 servings

1 Sprinkle chicken evenly with pepper. In 12-inch nonstick skillet or 6-quart Dutch oven, heat oil over medium-high heat. Add chicken. Cook for 4 to 6 minutes or just until brown on both sides. Reduce heat to low.

2 Combine peel, juice and honey in small bowl. Brush honey mixture on both sides of chicken pieces. Cover. Cook for 14 to 17 minutes, or until meat near bone is no longer pink and juices run clear.

Nutrition Facts	Amount/serving	%DV*	Amount/serving	%DV*
Serving Size 1/2 breast (91g)	Total Fat 4g	6%	Total Carbohydrate 4g	1%
Servings per Recipe 6	Saturated Fat <1g	5%	Dietary Fiber <1g	0%
Calories 152	Cholesterol 69mg	23%	Sugars 3g	
Calories from Fat 33	Sodium 60mg	3%	Protein 25g	

Vitamin A 0% • Vitamin C 6% • Calcium 2% • Iron 4%
*Percent Daily Values (DV) are based on a 2000 calorie diet.

Menu Planning Guide
One serving of this recipe provides:
1 Meat, Poultry & Fish

Diet Exchanges:
3 lean meat

Poultry

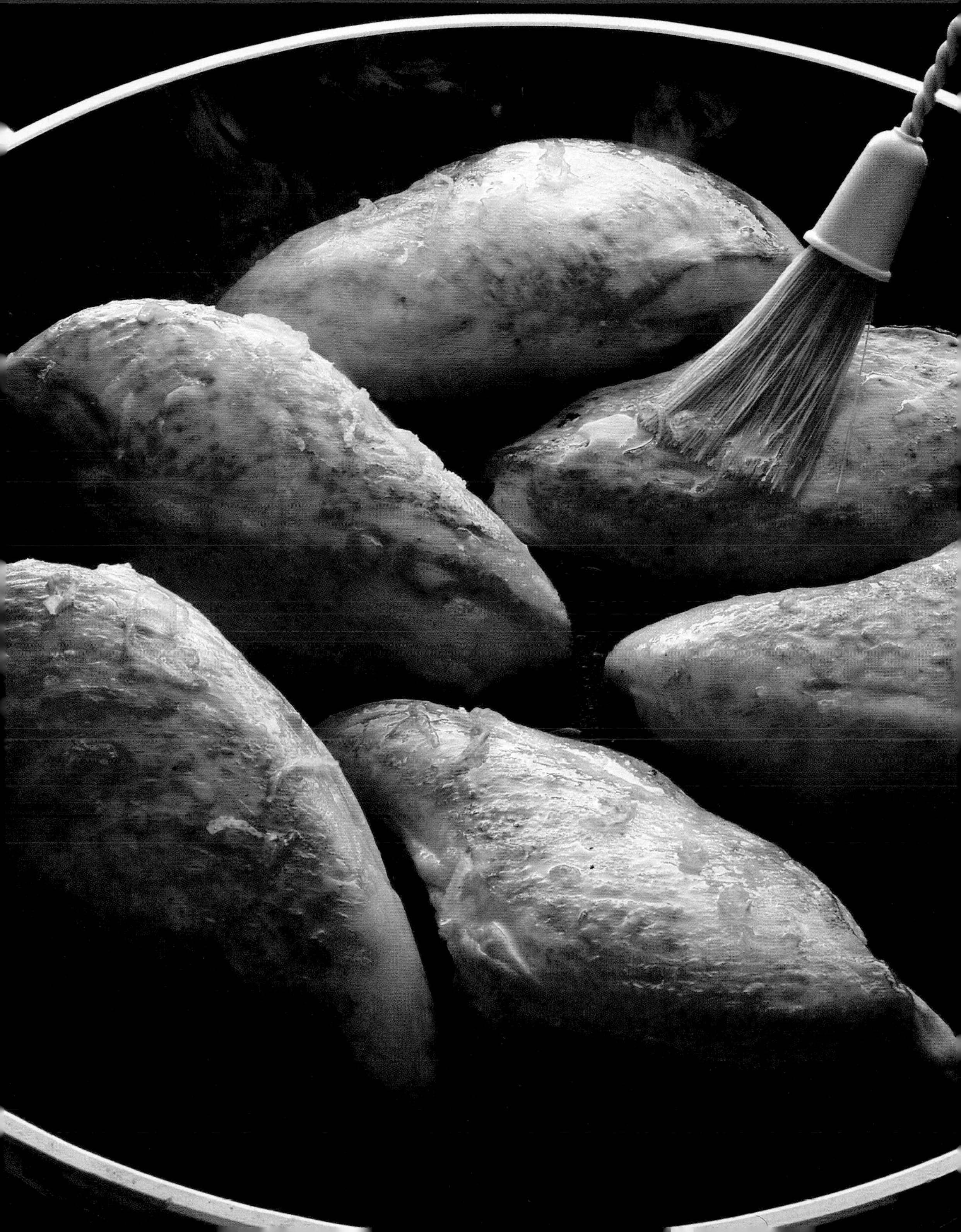

Tandoori Turkey & Rice

Serve with Tomato & Feta Pita Pizzas (p 87) or a crisp green salad

1 can (14½ oz.) ready-to-serve chicken broth
1 teaspoon chili powder
½ to 1 teaspoon ground cumin
¼ teaspoon ground turmeric
¼ teaspoon garlic powder
⅛ teaspoon white pepper
½ cups uncooked instant brown rice
1 lb. cooked turkey breast, cut into
    ½-inch cubes
½ cup red pepper strips (2 x ¼-inch strips)
1 medium carrot, thinly sliced (½ cup)
2 tablespoons snipped fresh cilantro or
    Italian parsley

servings

1 Combine broth, chili powder, cumin, turmeric, garlic powder and pepper in 12-inch nonstick skillet. Bring to boil over high heat. Stir in rice. Cover. Reduce heat to low. Simmer for 5 minutes.

2 Stir in turkey, red pepper and carrot. Re-cover. Simmer for additional 5 to 6 minutes, or until turkey is hot and liquid is absorbed. Remove from heat. Stir in cilantro.

Nutrition Facts	Amount/serving	%DV*	Amount/serving	%DV*
Serving Size 1 cup (245g)	Total Fat 2g	3%	Total Carbohydrate 25g	8%
Servings per Recipe 6	Saturated Fat 1g	3%	Dietary Fiber 2g	8%
Calories 208	Cholesterol 48mg	16%	Sugars 1g	
Calories from Fat 19	Sodium 266mg	11%	Protein 21g	

Vitamin A 60% • Vitamin C 35% • Calcium 2% • Iron 10%
*Percent Daily Values (DV) are based on a 2000 calorie diet.

Menu Planning Guide
One serving of this recipe provides:
1 Meat, Poultry & Fish
1 Bread, Cereal, Rice & Pasta

Diet Exchanges:
2 lean meat • 1½ starch

Turkey Saltimbocca

Serve with Mushrooms & Zucchini Persillade (p 75), Green Bean Sauté (p 70) or Hot Pasta Salad (p 98)

4 slices uncooked turkey breast (3 to 4 oz.
  each), pounded to ¼-inch thickness
1 tablespoon snipped fresh sage leaves
  Freshly ground pepper
12 slices fully cooked deli ham (⅓ oz. each)
¼ cup shredded fresh Parmesan cheese
½ cup dry white wine
4 whole fresh sage leaves

4 servings

Note: Saltimbocca is a Roman specialty traditionally made of thinly sliced veal and a thin slice of Italian ham sprinkled with sage. It is usually sautéed in butter, then braised in white wine.

1 Sprinkle turkey slices with snipped sage and pepper. Place 3 ham slices over each turkey slice. Secure ham with wooden pick.

2 Spray 12-inch nonstick skillet with non-stick vegetable cooking spray. Arrange turkey slices in skillet. Cook over medium heat for 15 to 18 minutes, or until browned on both sides and turkey is no longer pink. With ham side up, sprinkle Parmesan cheese evenly over turkey slices.

3 Increase heat to medium-high. Add wine to skillet. Cook for 2 to 3 minutes, or until cheese is melted and wine is slightly reduced. To serve, garnish with whole sage leaves and spoon reduced wine over turkey slices. Remove wooden picks before eating.

Nutrition Facts	Amount/serving	%DV*	Amount/serving	%DV*
Serving Size 1 slice (113g)	Total Fat 4g	6%	Total Carbohydrate 1g	0%
Servings per Recipe 4	Saturated Fat 2g	8%	Dietary Fiber 0g	0%
Calories 150	Cholesterol 72mg	24%	Sugars 1g	
Calories from Fat 32	Sodium 401mg	17%	Protein 27g	

Vitamin A 2% • Vitamin C 0% • Calcium 10% • Iron 10%
*Percent Daily Values (DV) are based on a 2000 calorie diet.

Menu Planning Guide
One serving of this recipe provides:
1 Meat, Poultry & Fish

Diet Exchanges:
3 lean meat

Chicken-filled Corn Bread Crepes

:rve with Rice with Beans & Jalapeños (p 104) or Spanish Rice (p 106)

:repes:

'4 *cups skim milk*

'4 *cup all-purpose flour*

'4 *cup frozen cholesterol-free egg product, defrosted; or 1 egg, beaten*

'4 *cup yellow cornmeal*

auce:

.2 *tablespoons margarine*

.3 *tablespoons all-purpose flour*

'2 *teaspoon ground cumin*

'2 *teaspoon paprika*

'4 *teaspoon salt*

'4 *teaspoon pepper*

'2 *cups skim milk*

:lling:

'2 *cups torn fresh spinach leaves*

'2 *cup chopped red pepper*

'2 *cup chopped yellow squash*

'4 *cup diagonally sliced green onions*

2 *cups shredded cooked chicken breast (no skin)*

1 *teaspoon ground coriander*

'4 *teaspoon ground cumin*

'4 *teaspoon salt*

:servings

1 Combine crepe ingredients in medium mixing bowl. Beat with whisk until batter is smooth. Spray 7-inch nonstick skillet with nonstick vegetable cooking spray. Heat skillet over medium heat. Add 3 scant tablespoons batter to skillet, tilting skillet to coat bottom. Cook for 45 seconds to 1 minute 15 seconds, or until crepe is lightly browned on both sides, turning crepe over after half the time. Repeat with remaining batter, stacking crepes between sheets of wax paper. (Spray skillet with nonstick vegetable cooking spray between crepes.) Set aside.

2 Melt margarine in 1-quart saucepan over medium heat. Stir in 3 tablespoons flour, 1/2 teaspoon cumin, the paprika, 1/4 teaspoon salt and the pepper. Blend in milk. Cook for 4 to 10 minutes, or until sauce thickens and bubbles, stirring constantly. Remove from heat. Cover to keep warm. Set aside.

3 Spray 10-inch nonstick skillet with nonstick vegetable cooking spray. Add spinach, red pepper, squash and onions. Cook over medium heat for 3 to 4 1/2 minutes, or until pepper is tender-crisp, stirring frequently. Stir in remaining filling ingredients. Cook for 1 to 2 minutes, or until hot, stirring frequently. Remove from heat. Stir in 1/3 cup sauce. Spoon about 1/4 cup filling down center of each crepe. Roll up. Spoon remaining sauce evenly over crepes.

Nutrition Facts	Amount/serving	%DV*	Amount/serving	%DV*
Serving Size 2 crepes with sauce (297g)	Total Fat 6g	8%	Total Carbohydrate 30g	10%
	Saturated Fat 1g	6%	Dietary Fiber 4g	14%
ervings per Recipe 6	Cholesterol 42mg	14%	Sugars 7g	
alories 263 Calories from Fat 50	Sodium 380mg	16%	Protein 24g	
	Vitamin A 110% • Vitamin C 60% • Calcium 25% • Iron 25%			
	*Percent Daily Values (DV) are based on a 2000 calorie diet.			

Menu Planning Guide

One serving of this recipe provides:

1/2 Milk, Yogurt & Cheese
 1 Meat, Poultry & Fish
1/2 Vegetable
 1 Bread, Cereal, Rice & Pasta

Diet Exchanges:

2 lean meat • 1/2 skim milk • 1 1/2 starch • 1/2 vegetable

Chinese-style Fish with Vegetables

Serve with Baked Eggrolls (p 63) or Spicy Chicken Wontons (p 40)

½ oz. dried shiitake mushrooms

½ cups hot water

½ lbs. cod fillets, cut into 1-inch pieces

½ teaspoon salt

1 egg white, beaten

3 tablespoons cornstarch

Sauce:

¼ cups reserved mushroom liquid

2 tablespoons low-sodium soy sauce

1 tablespoon rice wine vinegar

1 tablespoon dry sherry

1 tablespoon plus 1 teaspoon cornstarch

1 tablespoon sugar

1 teaspoon instant chicken bouillon granules

½ teaspoon sesame oil

½ cup water

1 tablespoon vegetable oil

1 clove garlic, minced

1 teaspoon grated fresh gingerroot

1 medium green pepper, cut into 1-inch pieces

1 medium red pepper, cut into 1-inch pieces

1 medium carrot, cut into 2 x ¼-inch strips
    (¾ cup)

1 small onion, cut into 12 wedges

½ cup diagonally sliced green onions
    (1½-inch lengths)

4 cups hot cooked white rice

servings

1 Place mushrooms in small mixing bowl. Pour hot water over mushrooms. Let soak for 30 minutes, or until softened. Drain liquid, reserving 1¼ cups. Slice mushrooms. Set aside.

2 Place fish in medium mixing bowl. Sprinkle with salt. Add egg white. Stir to coat. Sprinkle 3 tablespoons cornstarch over fish mixture. Toss to coat. Set aside.

3 Combine sauce ingredients in small mixing bowl. Set aside. In wok, heat ½ cup water over medium-high heat until boiling. Spray round cooking rack with nonstick vegetable cooking spray. Arrange fish on prepared rack. Set rack in wok about 1½ inches above water. Cover. Steam for 3 to 5 minutes, or until fish is firm and opaque and just begins to flake. Remove from heat. Set aside.

4 Drain and discard water from wok. Wipe wok with paper towel. In same wok, heat vegetable oil over high heat. Add garlic and gingerroot. Stir in prepared mushrooms and remaining ingredients, except rice. Cook for 3 to 4 minutes, or until onion is tender-crisp, stirring constantly. Add fish. Cook for 1 to 2 minutes, or until hot, stirring gently. Add sauce mixture. Cook for 1 to 2 minutes, or until sauce is thickened and translucent, stirring constantly. Serve over rice.

Nutrition Facts	Amount/serving	%DV*	Amount/serving	%DV*
Serving Size 1¼ cups (265g)	Total Fat 3g	4%	Total Carbohydrate 40g	13%
Servings per Recipe 8	Saturated Fat <1g	0%	Dietary Fiber 1g	4%
Calories 266	Cholesterol 36mg	12%	Sugars 3g	
Calories from Fat 26	Sodium 451mg	19%	Protein 19g	

Vitamin A 35% • Vitamin C 40% • Calcium 4% • Iron 10%
*Percent Daily Values (DV) are based on a 2000 calorie diet.

Menu Planning Guide

One serving of this recipe provides:
1 Meat, Poultry & Fish
1 Vegetable
2 Bread, Cereal, Rice & Pasta

Diet Exchanges:

2 lean meat • 2 starch • 1 vegetable

Multicolored Shells with Shrimp & Scallops

Serve with Caponata (p 66) and a crisp green salad

1½ cups uncooked multicolored medium
    pasta shells
½ cup ready-to-serve chicken broth
¼ cup dry sherry or water
1 tablespoon all-purpose flour
1 tablespoon lemon juice
½ teaspoon dried oregano leaves
½ teaspoon dried marjoram leaves
¼ teaspoon pepper
1 tablespoon margarine
8 oz. fresh mushrooms, sliced (3 cups)
½ cup diagonally sliced green onions
    (½-inch slices)
3 cloves garlic, minced
8 oz. fresh medium shrimp, shelled and
    deveined
8 oz. fresh bay scallops, rinsed and drained
    Shredded fresh Parmesan cheese (optional)

4 servings

1 Prepare shells as directed on package. Rinse and drain. Set aside. In 1-cup measure, combine broth, sherry, flour, juice, oregano, marjoram and pepper. Set aside.

2 Melt margarine in 10-inch nonstick skillet over medium-high heat. Add mushrooms, onions and garlic. Cook for 3½ to 5 minutes, or until mushrooms are tender, stirring frequently. Stir in broth mixture. Bring to boil, stirring constantly. Boil for 2 minutes.

3 Stir in shells, shrimp and scallops. Cook for 5 to 6½ minutes, or until shrimp and scallops are firm and opaque, stirring constantly. Sprinkle each serving with Parmesan cheese.

Nutrition Facts	Amount/serving	%DV*	Amount/serving	%DV*
Serving Size approximately 1 cup (298g)	Total Fat 5g	8%	Total Carbohydrate 33g	11%
	Saturated Fat 1g	5%	Dietary Fiber 3g	14%
Servings per Recipe 4	Cholesterol 75mg	25%	Sugars 2g	
Calories 264 Calories from Fat 48	Sodium 264mg	11%	Protein 19g	

Vitamin A 6% • Vitamin C 15% • Calcium 6% • Iron 25%
*Percent Daily Values (DV) are based on a 2000 calorie diet.

Menu Planning Guide

One serving of this recipe provides:
1 Meat, Poultry & Fish
1 Vegetable
1½ Bread, Cereal, Rice & Pasta

Diet Exchanges:

1 lean meat • 2 starch • 1 vegetable • ½ fat

Orange Scallops with Rice Noodles

Serve with steamed snow pea pods and Baked Eggrolls (p 63)

Sauce:

½ to 1 teaspoon grated orange peel

¼ cup fresh orange juice

2 teaspoons cornstarch

1½ teaspoons rice wine vinegar

½ to 1 teaspoon dried thyme leaves

½ teaspoon sugar

½ teaspoon salt

⅛ teaspoon pepper

4½ oz. uncooked rice noodles

2 teaspoons vegetable oil

1 medium onion, coarsely chopped (1 cup)

2 medium carrots, diagonally sliced (1 cup)

1 cup green pepper strips (2 x ¼-inch strips)

1 lb. fresh bay scallops, rinsed and drained

4 servings

1 Combine sauce ingredients in 1-cup measure. Set aside. Prepare rice noodles as directed on package.

2 Meanwhile, heat oil over high heat in wok or 12-inch nonstick skillet. Add onion, carrots and pepper strips. Cook for 3 to 5 minutes, or until vegetables are tender crisp, stirring constantly.

3 Add scallops. Cook for 3 to 5 minutes, or until scallops are firm and opaque, stirring constantly. Add sauce. Cook for 20 to 40 seconds, or until sauce thickens and bubbles, stirring constantly. Remove from heat. Drain noodles. Serve scallop mixture over noodles.

Nutrition Facts	Amount/serving	%DV*	Amount/serving	%DV*
Serving Size approximately 1¾ cups (298g) Servings per Recipe 4 Calories 230 Calories from Fat 39	Total Fat 4g	7%	Total Carbohydrate 37g	12%
	Saturated Fat 1g	4%	Dietary Fiber 3g	11%
	Cholesterol 18mg	6%	Sugars 8g	
	Sodium 519mg	22%	Protein 11g	

Vitamin A 190% • Vitamin C 70% • Calcium 4% • Iron 8%

*Percent Daily Values (DV) are based on a 2000 calorie diet.

Menu Planning Guide

One serving of this recipe provides:

1 Meat, Poultry & Fish
1½ Vegetable
1½ Bread, Cereal, Rice & Pasta

Diet Exchanges:

1 lean meat • 2 starch • 1½ vegetable

Shrimp Curry

Serve with a mixed green salad and a whole wheat dinner roll

¼ cup dry white wine

2 tablespoons vegetable oil

½ cup finely chopped shallots

½ cup finely chopped red pepper

2 tablespoons all-purpose flour

1 cup skim milk

1 tablespoon curry powder*

½ teaspoon salt

⅛ teaspoon cayenne

1 lb. cooked medium shrimp, shelled and
    deveined (no tails)

3 cups hot cooked long-grain white rice

1 to 2 tablespoons snipped fresh parsley
    Prepared mango chutney (optional)

servings

There are two basic types of curry powder: a standard version and a hotter version, known as "Madras."

1 Combine wine and oil in 12-inch nonstick skillet. Heat over medium heat until bubbly. Add shallots and chopped pepper. Cook for 2½ to 3½ minutes, or until vegetables are tender, stirring occasionally.

2 Stir in flour. Cook for 1 minute, stirring constantly. Gradually blend in milk with whisk. Stir in curry powder, salt and cayenne. Cook for 2 to 3 minutes, or until mixture thickens and bubbles, stirring constantly.

3 Stir in shrimp. Cook for 3 to 5 minutes, or until heated through, stirring frequently. Serve shrimp mixture over rice. Garnish with parsley. Serve chutney as a condiment with shrimp curry.

Nutrition Facts	Amount/serving	%DV*	Amount/serving	%DV*
Serving Size 1 cup (242g)	Total Fat 6g	9%	Total Carbohydrate 37g	12%
Servings per Recipe 6	Saturated Fat 1g	5%	Dietary Fiber 1g	5%
Calories 269	Cholesterol 109mg	36%	Sugars 3g	
Calories from Fat 51	Sodium 327mg	14%	Protein 17g	

Vitamin A 15% • Vitamin C 35% • Calcium 10% • Iron 20%

*Percent Daily Values (DV) are based on a 2000 calorie diet.

Menu Planning Guide
One serving of this recipe provides:
1 Meat, Poultry & Fish
1 Bread, Cereal, Rice & Pasta

Diet Exchanges:
1 lean meat • 2½ starch • ½ fat

Shrimp in Red Garlic Sauce

Serve with Sushi Sandwiches (p 91) or Baked Eggrolls (p 63)

Sauce:

3/4 cup spicy vegetable juice

1 tablespoon cornstarch

1 tablespoon sugar

1 tablespoon rice wine vinegar

1/8 teaspoon crushed red pepper flakes (optional)

1 stalk celery, chopped (1/2 cup)

2 teaspoons vegetable oil

2 cloves garlic, minced

1 pkg. (12 oz.) frozen cooked medium shrimp,
   defrosted and drained

1/4 cup diagonally sliced green onions

2 cups hot cooked white rice

4 servings

1 Combine sauce ingredients in 1-cup measure. Set aside. In 10-inch non-stick skillet, combine celery, oil and garlic. Cook over medium heat for 3½ to 5 minutes, or until celery is tender-crisp, stirring occasionally.

2 Add sauce mixture. Cook for 1½ to 2 minutes, or until sauce thickens and bubbles, stirring constantly.

3 Add shrimp and onions. Cook for additional 1½ to 3 minutes, or until shrimp is hot, stirring frequently. Serve over rice.

Nutrition Facts	Amount/serving	%DV*	Amount/serving	%DV*
	Total Fat 3g	5%	Total Carbohydrate 37g	12%
Serving Size approximately 1 cup (248g)	Saturated Fat 1g	3%	Dietary Fiber 1g	4%
Servings per Recipe 4	Cholesterol 131mg	44%	Sugars 5g	
Calories 255	Sodium 332mg	14%	Protein 17g	
Calories from Fat 31	Vitamin A 15% • Vitamin C 25% • Calcium 6% • Iron 20%			
	*Percent Daily Values (DV) are based on a 2000 calorie diet.			

Menu Planning Guide

One serving of this recipe provides:
1 Meat, Poultry & Fish
½ Vegetable
1 Bread, Cereal, Rice & Pasta

Diet Exchanges:

1½ lean meat • 2 starch • ½ vegetable

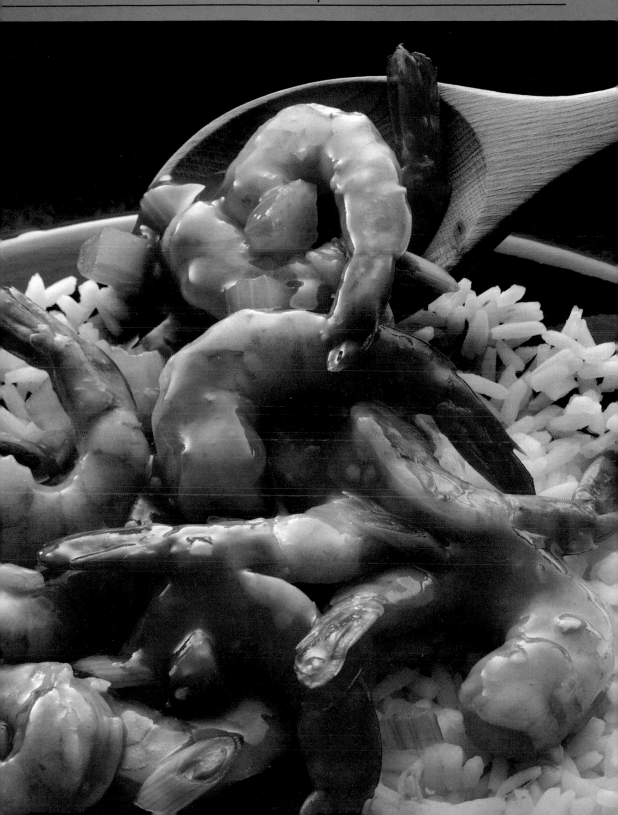

Vegetable Shrimp Stir-fry

Serve with hot cooked white rice and Spicy Chicken Wontons (p 40)
or Baked Eggrolls (p 63)

1 tablespoon vegetable oil

1 pkg. (9 oz.) frozen broccoli cuts

2 medium carrots, cut into 2 x ¼-inch
    strips (1 cup)

2 cloves garlic, minced

1 pkg. (10 oz.) frozen cooked medium shrimp,
    defrosted and drained

1 cup fresh snow pea pods

2 tablespoons reduced-sodium soy sauce

2 tablespoons water

1 tablespoon cornstarch

½ teaspoon grated fresh gingerroot

4 servings

1 Heat wok or 12-inch nonstick skillet over medium-high heat. Add oil, broccoli, carrot strips and garlic. Cook for 5 to 7 minutes, or until broccoli is defrosted, stirring frequently. Add shrimp and pea pods. Cook for 2 to 4 minutes, or until pea pods are bright green and mixture is hot, stirring frequently.

2 Combine remaining ingredients in 1-cup measure. Add to wok. Cook for 30 to 45 seconds, or until sauce is thickened and translucent, stirring constantly.

Nutrition Facts	Amount/serving	%DV*	Amount/serving	%DV*	Menu Planning Guide
Serving Size approximately 1 cup (237g)	Total Fat 5g	7%	Total Carbohydrate 13g	4%	One serving of this recipe provides:
	Saturated Fat 1g	4%	Dietary Fiber 3g	17%	1 Meat, Poultry & Fish
Servings per Recipe 4	Cholesterol 138mg	46%	Sugars 6g		1 Vegetable
Calories 166 Calories from Fat 40	Sodium 434mg	18%	Protein 19g		

Vitamin A 110% • Vitamin C 130% • Calcium 10% • Iron 20%
*Percent Daily Values (DV) are based on a 2000 calorie diet.

Diet Exchanges:
2 lean meat • ½ starch • 1 vegetable

Baked Eggrolls

Serve with Shrimp in Red Garlic Sauce (p 58), Hot & Spicy Pork Salad (p 18) or Jalapeño Curly Noodles (p 101)

1 cup hot water

½ oz. dried shiitake mushrooms

3 tablespoons cold water

1 tablespoon soy sauce

1 teaspoon cornstarch

2 teaspoons toasted sesame oil

4 cups finely shredded green cabbage

2 cups fresh bean sprouts

2 medium carrots, shredded (1 cup)

2 cloves garlic, minced

1 teaspoon grated fresh gingerroot

⅛ to ¼ teaspoon crushed red pepper flakes
    (optional)

6 eggroll skins (7-inch)

servings

1 Combine hot water and mushrooms in small mixing bowl. Let stand for 30 minutes. Drain, pressing mushrooms with back of spoon to release excess liquid. Remove and discard tough stems. Thinly slice mushrooms. Set aside.

2 Combine cold water, soy sauce and cornstarch in small bowl. Set aside. In 12-inch nonstick skillet, heat sesame oil over medium-high heat. Add cabbage, sprouts, carrots, garlic, gingerroot and pepper flakes. Cook for 5 to 7 minutes, or until cabbage is tender, stirring frequently. Stir in soy sauce mixture. Cook for 15 to 30 seconds, or until mixture thickens and bubbles, stirring constantly. Remove from heat. Stir in mushrooms. Let filling cool to room temperature.

3 Heat oven to 400°F. Spray baking sheet with nonstick vegetable cooking spray. Set aside. Spoon about ½ cup filling diagonally across 1 eggroll skin, just below center.

4 Brush top corner with water. Roll up eggroll skin, folding in sides to enclose filling. Place eggroll on prepared baking sheet. Repeat with remaining filling and eggroll skins. Spray eggrolls with nonstick vegetable cooking spray. Bake for 25 to 30 minutes, or until eggrolls are brown and crisp. Serve with hot mustard, wasabi horseradish sauce or additional soy sauce, if desired.

Nutrition Facts	Amount/serving	%DV*	Amount/serving	%DV*
Serving Size 1 eggroll (182g) Servings per Recipe 6 Calories 98 Calories from Fat 19	Total Fat 2g	3%	Total Carbohydrate 18g	6%
	Saturated Fat <1g	2%	Dietary Fiber 4g	14%
	Cholesterol 0mg	0%	Sugars 6g	
	Sodium 254mg	11%	Protein 4g	
	Vitamin A 120% • Vitamin C 50% • Calcium 6% • Iron 10%			
	*Percent Daily Values (DV) are based on a 2000 calorie diet.			

Menu Planning Guide
One serving of this recipe provides:
2 Vegetable
½ Bread, Cereal, Rice & Pasta

Diet Exchanges:
½ starch • 2 vegetable

Braised Celery Root

Serve with Beef Stroganoff (p 13) or Beef Bourguignonne (p 31)

1 teaspoon olive oil

1 teaspoon margarine or butter

2 medium celery roots, peeled, halved and
thinly sliced (3 cups)

2 cups frozen pearl onions, defrosted and
drained

2 medium carrots, cut into 2 x ¼-inch strips
(1 cup)

1 cup ready-to-serve chicken broth

2 teaspoons sugar

¼ teaspoon freshly ground pepper

2 tablespoons snipped fresh parsley

8 servings

1 Heat oil and margarine in 12-inch non-stick skillet over medium-high heat. Add celery roots. Cook for 5 to 6 minutes, or until celery roots are lightly browned, stirring occasionally. Add onions. Cook for 2 to 3 minutes, or until onions are lightly browned, stirring occasionally.

2 Stir in carrots, broth, sugar and pepper. Reduce heat to medium. Cover. Cook for 12 to 15 minutes, or until celery roots are tender and liquid is slightly reduced. Garnish with parsley.

Nutrition Facts	Amount/serving	%DV*	Amount/serving	%DV*	Menu Planning Guide
Serving Size ½ cup (155g)	Total Fat 1	2%	Total Carbohydrate 10g	3%	One serving of this recipe provides: 1½ Vegetable
Servings per Recipe 8	Saturated Fat 0g	0%	Dietary Fiber 4g	15%	
Calories 54	Cholesterol 0mg	0%	Sugars 4g		
Calories from Fat 13	Sodium 154mg	6%	Protein 1g		

Vitamin A 90% • Vitamin C 10% • Calcium 4% • Iron 4%
*Percent Daily Values (DV) are based on a 2000 calorie diet.

Diet Exchanges:
1½ vegetable

Caponata

Serve with Multicolored Shells with Shrimp & Scallops (p 52)
or Garbanzo Skillet Meal (p 97)

1 medium eggplant (1 lb.), cut crosswise into
    $1/2$-inch slices
2 teaspoons olive oil
1 small onion, chopped ($1/2$ cup)
$1/3$ cup sliced celery
$1/4$ cup red wine vinegar
1 clove garlic, minced
1 can ($14^1/2$ oz.) whole tomatoes, drained
    and cut up
$1/4$ cup halved pitted medium black olives
1 tablespoon capers, drained (optional)
1 teaspoon dried oregano leaves
$1/4$ teaspoon freshly ground pepper
$1/4$ cup toasted pine nuts (optional)
18 slices Italian bread, toasted
    Shredded fresh Parmesan cheese (optional)

18 servings

1 Heat oven to 500°F. Spray baking sheet with nonstick vegetable cooking spray. Arrange eggplant in single layer on prepare baking sheet. Brush both sides of eggplant with oil. Bake for 12 to 13 minutes, or until eggplant is golden brown. Cut slices into $1/4$-inch cubes. Set aside.

2 Combine onion, celery, vinegar and garlic in 2-quart saucepan. Cook over medium heat for $4^1/2$ to 6 minutes, or until onion is tender, stirring occasionally. Stir in tomatoes, olives, capers, oregano and pepper. Cook for additional $2^1/2$ to 4 minutes, or until mixture is hot and flavors are blended, stirring occasionally. Remove from heat. Stir in eggplant and nuts. Cool slightly.

3 Place caponata in medium mixing bowl. Cover with plastic wrap. Refrigerate overnight, stirring occasionally. To serve, sprinkle each slice bread with cheese and top with 3 tablespoons caponata.

Nutrition Facts	Amount/serving	%DV*	Amount/serving	%DV*
Serving Size 1 slice (88g)	Total Fat 2g	3%	Total Carbohydrate 18g	6%
Servings per Recipe 18	Saturated Fat <1g	2%	Dietary Fiber 2g	8%
Calories 101	Cholesterol 0mg	0%	Sugars 3g	
Calories from Fat 17	Sodium 234mg	10%	Protein 3g	
	Vitamin A 4% • Vitamin C 8% • Calcium 4% • Iron 6%			
	*Percent Daily Values (DV) are based on a 2000 calorie diet.			

Menu Planning Guide
One serving of this recipe provides:
  $1/2$ Vegetable
  1 Bread, Cereal, Rice & Pasta

Diet Exchanges:
1 starch • $1/2$ vegetable

Cool Tarragon Cucumbers

*Serve with Country French Skillet Dinner (p 34)
or Peppercorn Pork Tenderloin (p 21)*

2 medium cucumbers, sliced (4 cups)
1 medium red onion, thinly sliced and
   separated into rings

Dressing:

2 cup plain low-fat or nonfat yogurt
2 tablespoons to ¼ cup fresh tarragon leaves
2 tablespoons cider vinegar
2 tablespoons sugar
4 teaspoon salt

Servings

1 Combine cucumbers and onion in large mixing bowl or salad bowl. Set aside. In small mixing bowl, combine dressing ingredients. Stir until sugar is dissolved. Pour dressing over cucumber mixture. Toss to coat. Chill 1 hour to blend flavors. Serve on lettuce-lined plates.

Nutrition Facts	Amount/serving	%DV*	Amount/serving	%DV*
Serving Size approximately ½ cup (90g) Servings per Recipe 8 Calories 41 Calories from Fat 4	Total Fat <1g	1%	Total Carbohydrate 8g	3%
	Saturated Fat <1g	1%	Dietary Fiber 1g	4%
	Cholesterol <1mg	0%	Sugars 7g	
	Sodium 80mg	3%	Protein 2g	
	Vitamin A 4% • Vitamin C 6% • Calcium 6% • Iron 4%			
	*Percent Daily Values (DV) are based on a 2000 calorie diet.			

Menu Planning Guide

One serving of this recipe provides:
1 Vegetable

Diet Exchanges:

1 vegetable

Green Bean Sauté

Serve with Beef Bourguignonne (p 31), Spring Lemon Chicken (p 42)
or Turkey Saltimbocca (p 46)

¼ cup hot ready-to-serve chicken broth

2 tablespoons snipped dry-pack sun-dried
tomatoes

¼ teaspoon dried bouquet garni

1 teaspoon olive oil

1 pkg. (9 oz.) frozen cut green beans,
defrosted and drained

4 oz. fresh whole oyster mushrooms (about
1¾ cups)

1 clove garlic, minced

⅛ to ¼ teaspoon crushed red pepper flakes

4 servings

1 Combine broth, tomatoes and bouquet
garni in small bowl. Let stand for 10
minutes. In 12-inch nonstick skillet, heat
oil over medium-high heat. Add beans,
mushrooms and garlic. Cook for 6 to 8
minutes, or until mixture is hot and mushrooms are tender, stirring frequently.

2 Add broth mixture to skillet. Cook for
seconds to 1 minute, or until liquid is
completely absorbed, stirring frequently.
Remove from heat. Sprinkle with red pepper flakes. Serve immediately.

Nutrition Facts	Amount/serving	%DV*	Amount/serving	%DV*
Serving Size approximately ¾ cup (101g)	Total Fat 2g	2%	Total Carbohydrate 7g	2%
	Saturated Fat <1g	1%	Dietary Fiber 2g	10%
Servings per Recipe 4	Cholesterol 0mg	0%	Sugars 2g	
Calories 44	Sodium 86mg	4%	Protein 2g	
Calories from Fat 14	Vitamin A 6% • Vitamin C 15% • Calcium 4% • Iron 6%			
	*Percent Daily Values (DV) are based on a 2000 calorie diet.			

Menu Planning Guide

One serving of this recipe provides:

1½ Vegetable

Diet Exchanges:

1½ vegetable

Hot Spinach Toss

Serve with Artichoke Turkey Hash (p 33) or roasted pork loin

2 teaspoons olive oil

8 oz. fresh mushrooms, quartered (3 cups)

½ large red onion, cut into ¼-inch wedges
   (2 cups)

2 tablespoons red wine vinegar

1 tablespoon sugar

1 teaspoon caraway seed (optional)

8 cups coarsely torn fresh spinach leaves

servings

1 Heat oil in 6-quart Dutch oven or stock-pot over medium-high heat. Add mushrooms. Cook for 8 to 10 minutes, or until mushrooms are lightly browned, stirring frequently. Add onion. Cook for 5 to 6 minutes, or until onion is tender-crisp, stirring frequently.

2 Stir in vinegar, sugar and caraway seed. Remove from heat. Add spinach. Toss to combine. Serve immediately.

Nutrition Facts	Amount/serving	%DV*	Amount/serving	%DV*
Serving Size approximately ½ cup (116g)	Total Fat 2g	2%	Total Carbohydrate 7	2%
	Saturated Fat <1g	1%	Dietary Fiber 3g	10%
	Cholesterol 0mg	0%	Sugars 4g	
Servings per Recipe 8	Sodium 49mg	2%	Protein 2g	
Calories 47 Calories from Fat 14	Vitamin A 80% • Vitamin C 30% • Calcium 6% • Iron 10%			
	*Percent Daily Values (DV) are based on a 2000 calorie diet.			

Menu Planning Guide
One serving of this recipe provides:
1½ Vegetable

Diet Exchanges:
1½ vegetable

Mushrooms & Zucchini Persillade

Serve with Turkey Saltimbocca (p 46)
or Peppercorn Pork Tenderloin (p 21)

1 *teaspoon olive oil*

8 *oz. assorted fresh mushrooms (crimini,*
    shiitake, button), quartered (3 cups)

3 *medium zucchini, cut diagonally into*
    ½-inch slices (3 cups)

2 *tablespoons snipped fresh Italian parsley*

2 *cloves garlic, minced*

½ *teaspoon salt*

¼ *teaspoon pepper*

servings

Note: Persillade is the French term for a mixture
of parsley and garlic. It is a fresh way to season
simply prepared foods, such as vegetables, fish
and meat.

1 Heat oil in 10-inch nonstick skillet over medium heat. Add mushrooms and zucchini. Cook for 4 to 6 minutes, or until mushrooms are tender, stirring occasionally.

2 Stir in remaining ingredients. Cook for 2 to 3 minutes, or until zucchini is tender-crisp, stirring frequently. Serve immediately.

Nutrition Facts	Amount/serving	%DV*	Amount/serving	%DV*
Serving Size ½ cup (78g)	Total Fat 1g	1%	Total Carbohydrate 3g	1%
	Saturated Fat <1g	1%	Dietary Fiber 1g	4%
Servings per Recipe 8	Cholesterol 0mg	0%	Sugars 1g	
Calories 21	Sodium 136mg	6%	Protein 1g	
Calories from Fat 6	Vitamin A 4% • Vitamin C 10% • Calcium 2% • Iron 2%			
	*Percent Daily Values (DV) are based on a 2000 calorie diet.			

Menu Planning Guide
One serving of this recipe provides:
1 Vegetable

Diet Exchanges:
1 vegetable

Orange-gingered Acorn Squash

Serve with Hearty Beef Skillet Meal (p 14) or grilled turkey breast

1 acorn squash (about 1½ lbs.)

1 tablespoon frozen orange juice concentrate, defrosted

1 tablespoon honey

½ teaspoon ground ginger

¼ cup water

  Ground cinnamon

2 slices orange, quartered

4 servings

1 Heat oven to 350°F. Cut squash lengthwise into quarters. Remove seeds. Arrange quarters cut-sides-up in 10-inch square casserole. Pierce cut side of each quarter in several places with fork.

2 Combine concentrate, honey and ginger in small bowl. Brush juice mixture evenly over quarters.

3 Pour water into bottom of casserole. Cover. Bake for 40 to 45 minutes, or unti squash is tender. Let stand, covered, for 5 minutes. To serve, sprinkle lightly with cinnamon and garnish with quartered orange slices.

Microwave tip: Prepare as directed, except omit water. Microwave, covered, at High for 8 to 10 minutes, or until squash is tender, rotating casserole once.

Nutrition Facts

Serving Size
  ¼ squash (153g)
Servings
  per Recipe 4
Calories 103
  Calories
  from Fat 2

Amount/serving	%DV*	Amount/serving	%DV*
Total Fat <1g	0%	Total Carbohydrate 27g	9%
Saturated Fat <1g	0%	Dietary Fiber 6g	24%
Cholesterol 0mg	0%	Sugars 11g	
Sodium 6mg	0%	Protein 2g	

Vitamin A 10% • Vitamin C 40% • Calcium 6% • Iron 8%
*Percent Daily Values (DV) are based on a 2000 calorie diet.

Menu Planning Guide

One serving of this recipe provides:

1 Vegetable

Diet Exchanges:

1½ starch

Spicy Moroccan Vegetables

Serve with Ragout of Lamb (p 24) or Tandoori Turkey & Rice (p 45)

1 medium onion, chopped (1 cup)

1 medium turnip, cut into ¼-inch cubes
  (1 cup)

2 medium carrots, thinly sliced (1 cup)

2 tablespoons olive oil

2 cloves garlic, minced

1½ teaspoons ground cumin

½ teaspoon pepper

¼ teaspoon salt

1 medium red pepper, seeded and cut into
  1-inch chunks (1 cup)

1 medium zucchini, thinly sliced (1 cup)

1 can (16 oz.) garbanzo beans, rinsed and
  drained

1 cup raisins

3 tablespoons snipped fresh parsley

6 servings

1 Combine onion, turnip, carrots, oil, garlic, cumin, pepper and salt in 10-inch nonstick skillet. Cook over medium-high heat for 6 to 7 minutes, or until vegetables are tender-crisp, stirring occasionally.

2 Stir in red pepper and zucchini. Cook for 2 to 3 minutes, or until tender-crisp, stirring occasionally. Stir in beans, raisins and parsley. Cook for 2 to 3 minutes, or until hot, stirring occasionally.

Nutrition Facts	Amount/serving	%DV*	Amount/serving	%DV*
Serving Size approximately ½ cup (209g) Servings per Recipe 6	Total Fat 7g	10%	Total Carbohydrate 46g	15%
	Saturated Fat <1g	4%	Dietary Fiber 7g	30%
	Cholesterol 0mg	0%	Sugars 24g	
Calories 258 Calories from Fat 59	Sodium 123mg	5%	Protein 8g	
	Vitamin A 80% • Vitamin C 80% • Calcium 8% • Iron 20%			
	*Percent Daily Values (DV) are based on a 2000 calorie diet.			

Menu Planning Guide

One serving of this recipe provides:
1 Vegetable
1 Fruit

Diet Exchanges:

1½ starch • 1 vegetable • 1 fruit • 1 fat

Stir-fry Veggies in Wonton Baskets

Serve with Spicy Chicken Wontons (p 40),
Baked Eggrolls (p 63) or Fresh Spring Rolls (p 94)

5 wonton skins

...uce:

1 tablespoon water

1 tablespoon low-sodium soy sauce

2 teaspoons rice wine vinegar

1 teaspoon sugar

2 teaspoon grated fresh gingerroot

2 teaspoon cornstarch

2 teaspoons toasted sesame oil

1 medium carrot, thinly sliced (½ cup)

1 small onion, chopped (½ cup)

2 cup finely chopped red pepper

2 oz. fresh pea pods, cut in half crosswise
   (½ cup)

2 cup thinly sliced yellow summer squash,
   cut into quarters

4 cup sliced green onions
   Sesame seed

...ervings

*...: Wonton baskets can be made in advance.
...re cooled baskets in airtight container in a
...l, dry place.*

1 Heat oven to 350°F. Spray 8 cups of a 12-cup muffin pan with nonstick vegetable cooking spray. Spray 1 wonton skin with nonstick vegetable cooking spray. Place second wonton skin at 45° angle over first. Spray with nonstick vegetable cooking spray. Press skins in bottom and up sides of 1 prepared muffin cup, leaving tips pointed up. Repeat with remaining wonton skins.

2 Bake for 10 to 12 minutes, or until tips of wonton skins are golden brown. Transfer wonton baskets to wire rack to cool. In small bowl, combine sauce ingredients. Set aside.

3 Heat oil in 10-inch nonstick skillet over medium-high heat. Add carrot and chopped onion. Cook for 2 to 2½ minutes, or until vegetables are tender-crisp, stirring constantly. Add pepper, pea pods, squash and green onions. Cook for 1½ to 2 minutes, or until pea pods brighten in color, stirring constantly.

4 Stir in sauce. Cook for 20 to 30 seconds, or until sauce is thickened and translucent, stirring constantly. Spoon about ¼ cup vegetable mixture into each wonton basket. Sprinkle with sesame seed. Serve immediately.

Nutrition Facts	Amount/serving	%DV*	Amount/serving	%DV*	Menu Planning Guide
...rving Size ... baskets (147g) ...rvings ...er Recipe 4 ...lories 158 Calories ...rom Fat 28	Total Fat 3g	5%	Total Carbohydrate 28g	9%	One serving of this recipe provides: 1 Vegetable 1 Bread, Cereal, Rice & Pasta
	Saturated Fat 1g	3%	Dietary Fiber 2g	9%	
	Cholesterol 3mg	1%	Sugars 6g		
	Sodium 343mg	14%	Protein 5g		
	Vitamin A 110% • Vitamin C 70% • Calcium 4% • Iron 10%				**Diet Exchanges:** 1½ starch • 1 vegetable
	Percent Daily Values (DV) are based on a 2000 calorie diet.				

Summer Squash Scramble

Serve with Beef Bourguignonne (p 31) or any grilled meat

1 *medium onion, coarsely chopped (1 cup)*

1 *clove garlic, minced*

2 *teaspoons olive oil*

2 *medium zucchini squash, cut into ¼-inch slices (2 cups)*

1 *medium yellow squash, cut into ¼-inch slices (1 cup)*

½ *teaspoon dried basil leaves*

¼ *teaspoon salt*

2 *medium tomatoes, chopped (2 cups)*

1 *to 2 tablespoons grated Parmesan cheese (optional)*

8 servings

1 Combine onion, garlic and oil in 10-inc nonstick skillet. Cook over medium-hig heat for 2 to 3 minutes, or until onion is tender, stirring frequently.

2 Add squashes, basil and salt. Cook for to 7 minutes, or until squashes are tend crisp, stirring constantly.

3 Stir in tomatoes. Cook for 1 to 2 minut or until hot, stirring constantly. Remov from heat. Sprinkle with Parmesan cheese

Nutrition Facts	Amount/serving	%DV*	Amount/serving	%DV*
Serving Size approximately ½ cup (103g)	Total Fat 1g	2%	Total Carbohydrate 6g	2%
	Saturated Fat <1g	1%	Dietary Fiber 1g	4%
Servings per Recipe 8	Cholesterol 0mg	0%	Sugars 3g	
Calories 37	Sodium 72mg	3%	Protein 1g	
Calories from Fat 12	Vitamin A 15% • Vitamin C 25% • Calcium 2% • Iron 2%			

*Percent Daily Values (DV) are based on a 2000 calorie diet.

Menu Planning Guide

One serving of this recipe provides:

1 Vegetable

Diet Exchanges:

1 vegetable

Sweet-spiced Brussels Sprouts & Apples

Serve with Beef Stroganoff (p 13) or roast turkey

tablespoon honey

teaspoon ground nutmeg

cups water

lb. fresh Brussels sprouts, trimmed and
cut in half

medium red cooking apple, cored and cut
into ½-inch cubes (1½ cups)

teaspoon margarine

servings

1 Combine honey and nutmeg in small bowl. Set aside. In 2-quart saucepan, bring water to boil over high heat. Add sprouts. Return to boil. Cover.

2 Reduce heat to medium-low. Cook for 5 to 7 minutes, or until sprouts are tender. Drain. Add honey mixture, apple and margarine. Mix well. Cover. Let stand for 5 minutes, or until apple is hot.

Microwave tip: Reduce water to ¼ cup. In 2-quart casserole, combine sprouts and water. Cover. Microwave at High for 6 to 8 minutes, or until tender-crisp, stirring once or twice. Drain. Add honey mixture, apple and margarine. Mix well. Re-cover. Microwave at High for 1½ to 3 minutes, or until sprouts are tender and apple is hot.

Nutrition Facts	Amount/serving	%DV*	Amount/serving	%DV*
Serving Size ¾ cup (154g) Servings per Recipe 4 Calories 90 Calories from Fat 15	Total Fat 2g	3%	Total Carbohydrate 20g	7%
	Saturated Fat <1g	2%	Dietary Fiber 6g	23%
	Cholesterol 0mg	0%	Sugars 13g	
	Sodium 35mg	1%	Protein 3g	
	Vitamin A 10% • Vitamin C 120% • Calcium 4% • Iron 8%			
	*Percent Daily Values (DV) are based on a 2000 calorie diet.			

Menu Planning Guide
One serving of this recipe provides:
1 Vegetable

Diet Exchanges:
1 starch • 1 vegetable • 1 fruit

Tomato & Feta Pita Pizzas†

rve with Garbanzo Skillet Meal (p 97) or Tandoori Turkey & Rice (p 45)

3 *Roma tomatoes, finely chopped*
1 *tablespoon crumbled feta cheese*
1 *green onion, finely chopped*
2 *teaspoons balsamic vinegar*
1 *teaspoon olive oil*
4 *teaspoon dried oregano leaves*
4 *teaspoon pepper*
4 *whole soft pitas*

ervings

Combine all ingredients, except pitas, in small mixing bowl. Cover with plastic ap. Let stand for 20 minutes.

Heat oven to 350°F. Arrange pitas on baking sheet. Spread tomato mixture evenly er pitas. Bake for 10 to 12 minutes, or until t. Cut each pita into 4 wedges to serve.

: These pizzas can also be served as a ain dish.

riations:

3Q Chicken Pita Pizzas

1 *cup cubed cooked chicken breast (no skin; 1/2-inch cubes)*
4 *cup prepared barbecue sauce*
4 *whole soft pitas*
4 *cup shredded reduced-fat Cheddar cheese*

1 Heat oven to 350°F. In small mixing bowl, combine chicken and barbecue sauce. Set aside.

2 Arrange pitas on baking sheet. Spread chicken mixture evenly over pitas. Sprinkle cheese evenly over top. Bake for 10 to 12 minutes, or until pitas are hot and cheese is melted.

Carmelized Onion Pita Pizzas

1/2 *cup ready-to-serve chicken broth, divided*
1 *large onion, sliced into 1/4-inch rings*
4 *whole soft pitas*
1 *tablespoon plus 1 teaspoon shredded fresh Parmesan cheese*
1 *teaspoon snipped fresh rosemary leaves*

1 Heat 1/4 cup broth in 10-inch nonstick skillet over medium-low heat until bubbly. Add onion. Cook for 35 to 40 minutes, or until onion is dark golden brown, stirring occasionally. Sprinkle only enough of remaining 1/4 cup broth over onion as needed to prevent burning. (Adding too much broth at one time will make onions soggy and prevent browning.)

2 Heat oven to 350°F. Arrange pitas on baking sheet. Spread onion evenly over pitas. Sprinkle cheese and rosemary evenly over top. Bake for 10 to 12 minutes, or until pitas are hot and cheese is melted.

Nutrition acts	Amount/serving	%DV*	Amount/serving	%DV*	Menu Planning Guide
rving Size 2 wedges (59g) rvings er Recipe 8	Total Fat 1g	2%	Total Carbohydrate 18g	6%	One serving of this recipe provides: 1 Bread, Cereal, Rice & Pasta
	Saturated Fat 1<g	2%	Dietary Fiber 1g	3%	
alories 99	Cholesterol 2mg	0%	Sugars 1g		
Calories from Fat 13	Sodium 184mg	8%	Protein 3g		
	Vitamin A 4% • Vitamin C 8% • Calcium 4% • Iron 6%				
	*Percent Daily Values (DV) are based on a 2000 calorie diet.				Diet Exchanges: 1 starch

87

Veggie-stuffed Zucchini

Serve with Peppercorn Pork Tenderloin (p 21)
or Artichoke Turkey Hash (p 33)

3 *medium zucchini (5 oz. each)*
1½ *teaspoons margarine*
⅓ *cup chopped onion*
2 *cloves garlic, minced*
1 *cup chopped fresh mushrooms*
1 *medium tomato, chopped (1 cup)*

1 *tablespoon unseasoned dry bread crumbs*
¼ *teaspoon dried chervil leaves*
⅛ *teaspoon pepper*
3 *tablespoons shredded fresh Parmesan*
   cheese (optional)

6 servings

1 Heat oven to 375°F. Cut zucchini in half lengthwise. Scoop out pulp, leaving ¼-inch shells. Coarsely chop pulp. Set shells and pulp aside.

2 Melt margarine in 10-inch nonstick skillet over medium heat. Stir in onion and garlic. Cook for 2 to 3 minutes, or until onion is tender-crisp, stirring occasionally. Add reserved pulp and mushrooms to skillet. Cook for 2 to 3 minutes, or until pulp is tender-crisp, stirring frequently. Remove from heat. Stir in tomato, crumbs, chervil and pepper.

3 Spoon mixture evenly in shells. Arrange stuffed zucchini in 11 x 7-inch baking dish. Cover with foil. Bake for 25 to 30 minutes, until shells are tender-crisp. Sprinkle with Parmesan cheese. Let stand for 5 minutes before serving.

Nutrition Facts	Amount/serving	%DV*	Amount/serving	%DV*
Serving Size ½ zucchini (118g) Servings per Recipe 6 Calories 35 Calories from Fat 12	Total Fat 1g	2%	Total Carbohydrate 6g	2%
	Saturated Fat <1g	1%	Dietary Fiber 2g	6%
	Cholesterol 0mg	0%	Sugars 3g	
	Sodium 26mg	1%	Protein 2g	

Vitamin A 8% • Vitamin C 20% • Calcium 2% • Iron 4%
*Percent Daily Values (DV) are based on a 2000 calorie diet.

Menu Planning Guide
One serving of this recipe provides:
1 Vegetable

Diet Exchanges:
1 vegetable

Sushi Sandwiches

Serve with Gingered Turkey Stir-fry (p 36)
or Shrimp in Red Garlic Sauce (p 58)

2 cups uncooked short-grain white Japanese rice

3 tablespoons rice wine vinegar

2 cup fresh beet strips (1½ x ¼-inch strips)

¼ cup plus 2 teaspoons water, divided

2 teaspoons wasabi horseradish powder

8 sheets dried nori seaweed (8 x 7½-inch sheets)

2 cup peeled seeded cucumber strips (1½ x
    ¼-inch strips)

2 cup white radish strips (1½ x ¼-inch strips)

2 cup carrot strips (1½ x ¼-inch strips)

2 cup sliced green onions (1½ x ¼-inch
    lengths), quartered lengthwise

servings

1 Prepare rice as directed on package. Stir in vinegar. Cool completely, stirring occasionally. Set aside. In 1-quart saucepan, combine beets and ¼ cup water. Cover. Cook over high heat for 5 to 7½ minutes, or until tender. Drain. Cool completely. Set aside. In small bowl, combine horseradish powder and remaining 2 teaspoons water. Stir until smooth paste forms. Set horseradish aside.

2 Place 1 sheet seaweed shiny-side-down on sushi mat or wax paper. Spread about 1 cup rice evenly over seaweed, leaving 1-inch margin on one long side of seaweed. Spread ¼ to ½ teaspoon horseradish lengthwise across center.

3 Arrange 5 strips beet end-to-end lengthwise across center. Repeat with 5 strips cucumber, 5 strips radish and 5 strips carrot. Arrange 1 tablespoon green onions evenly over other vegetables.

4 Roll up tightly, peeling back sushi mat while rolling. Press ends to seal. Slice rolls crosswise into eight 1-inch pieces, rinsing knife with water after each cut. Repeat with remaining ingredients. Serve with additional low-sodium soy sauce, if desired.

Nutrition Facts	Amount/serving	%DV*	Amount/serving	%DV*
Serving Size 8 pieces (1 roll) (234g)	Total Fat <1g	0%	Total Carbohydrate 58g	19%
Servings per Recipe 8	Saturated Fat <1g	1%	Dietary Fiber 2g	8%
Calories 270	Cholesterol 0mg	0%	Sugars 2g	
Calories from Fat 4	Sodium 11mg	0%	Protein 6g	

Vitamin A 50% • Vitamin C 15% • Calcium 2% • Iron 4%
*Percent Daily Values (DV) are based on a 2000 calorie diet.

Menu Planning Guide
One serving of this recipe provides:
½ Vegetable
2 Bread, Cereal, Rice & Pasta

Diet Exchanges:
3½ starch • ½ vegetable

Basmati & Wild Rice with Fennel

Serve with Lemon Chicken & Vegetables (p 39)
or Mediterranean Pot Stickers (p 103)

2 cups water

1/2 cup uncooked wild rice

1 tablespoon olive oil

1 medium onion, chopped (1 cup)

1 cup chopped fennel bulb

2 cloves garlic, minced

1 cup uncooked Basmati or long-grain
　white rice

1 1/2 cups ready-to-serve chicken broth

1 teaspoon grated lemon peel

1/4 cup snipped fresh parsley

2 tablespoons slivered almonds (optional)

1/4 teaspoon salt

1/4 teaspoon freshly ground pepper

12 servings

1 Combine water and wild rice in 2-quart saucepan. Bring to boil over high heat. Reduce heat to low. Cover. Simmer for 30 35 minutes, or until rice is tender and kernels are open. Drain.

2 Meanwhile, heat oil in 3-quart saucepa over medium heat. Add onion, fennel and garlic. Cook for 4 to 6 minutes, or un vegetables are tender, stirring frequently. Stir in Basmati rice. Cook for 1 minute, stir ring constantly. Add broth and peel. Bring to boil over high heat. Reduce heat to low. Cover. Simmer for 13 to 15 minutes, or un rice is tender and liquid is absorbed.

3 Remove from heat. Stir in wild rice, parsley, almonds, salt and pepper. Recover. Let stand for 5 minutes. Fluff with fork before serving.

Nutrition Facts	Amount/serving	%DV*	Amount/serving	%DV*
Serving Size 1/2 cup (191g)	Total Fat 2g	3%	Total Carbohydrate 28	9%
	Saturated Fat <1g	2%	Dietary Fiber 1g	5%
Servings per Recipe 12	Cholesterol 0mg	0%	Sugars 1g	
Calories 141	Sodium 149mg	6%	Protein 4g	
Calories from Fat 15	Vitamin A 2% • Vitamin C 6% • Calcium 2% • Iron 6%			
	*Percent Daily Values (DV) are based on a 2000 calorie diet.			

Menu Planning Guide
One serving of this recipe provides:
1 Bread, Cereal, Rice & Pasta

Diet Exchanges:
1 1/2 starch

Fresh Spring Rolls

Serve with Jalapeño Curly Noodles (p 101)
or Stir-fry Veggies in Wonton Baskets (p 81)

2 cups water

1 oz. uncooked cellophane noodles

1/2 lb. ground chicken (breast meat only; no skin), crumbled

2 tablespoons sliced green onion

1 medium carrot, shredded (1/2 cup)

1 tablespoon soy sauce

1/4 teaspoon white pepper

12 round rice paper sheets (8 1/2-inch)*

24 sprigs fresh cilantro

24 whole fresh spinach leaves

Plum sauce (optional)

12 servings

Rice paper sheets may be purchased in Oriental or specialty food stores. If 8 1/2-inch rice paper sheets are unavailable, use bowl with 8 1/2-inch diameter as template on larger sheets and cut circles of correct size.

1 Bring water to boil in 2-quart saucepan over high heat. Add noodles. Cook for 2 to 3 minutes, or until tender, stirring occasionally. Drain. With scissors, cut noodles 1-inch lengths. Set aside.

2 Combine chicken and onion in 10-inch nonstick skillet. Cook over medium heat for 3 1/2 to 5 minutes, or until meat is no longer pink, stirring occasionally. Drain. Stir in noodles, carrot, soy sauce and pepper. Set meat mixture aside.

3 Wet both sides of each rice paper sheet by holding briefly under cold running water. Place wet rice paper sheets on flat work surface. Cover with dampened paper towels to prevent drying.

4 Remove 1 sheet. Place 2 sprigs cilantro just below center. Top with 2 tablespoon meat mixture and 2 spinach leaves. Roll up folding in sides. Repeat with remaining sheets, cilantro, meat mixture and spinach leaves. Cover rolls with plastic wrap. Chill until serving time. Serve with plum sauce.

Nutrition Facts	Amount/serving	%DV*	Amount/serving	%DV*
Serving Size 1 roll (72g)	Total Fat 1g	2%	Total Carbohydrate 23g	8%
Servings per Recipe 12	Saturated Fat <1g	1%	Dietary Fiber <1g	2%
Calories 136	Cholesterol 15mg	5%	Sugars 0g	
Calories from Fat 10	Sodium 304mg	13%	Protein 8g	
	Vitamin A 35% • Vitamin C 4% • Calcium 2% • Iron 10%			
	*Percent Daily Values (DV) are based on a 2000 calorie diet.			

Menu Planning Guide
One serving of this recipe provides:
1 1/2 Bread, Cereal, Rice & Pasta

Diet Exchanges:
1/2 lean meat • 1 1/2 starch

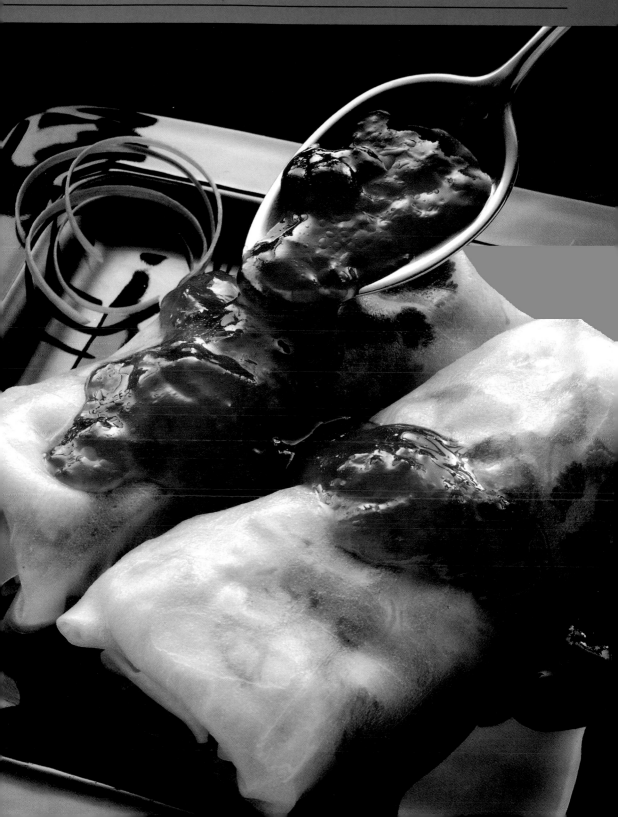

Garbanzo Skillet Meal

Serve with Tomato & Feta Pita Pizza (p 87) or Caponata (p 66)

1 cup boiling water

¼ cup uncooked bulgur (cracked wheat)

1 cup red and green pepper chunks
(1-inch chunks)

1 small onion, thinly sliced and separated
into rings

1 medium carrot or parsnip, shredded
(½ cup)

1 teaspoon olive oil

1 can (15 oz.) garbanzo beans, rinsed
and drained

1 can (8 oz.) tomato sauce

1 small yellow squash, halved lengthwise
and sliced (½ cup)

1 teaspoon dried oregano leaves

½ teaspoon grated lemon peel

½ teaspoon dried dill weed

⅛ teaspoon pepper

servings

1 Combine water and bulgur in small mixing bowl. Let stand for 30 minutes. Drain, pressing with back of spoon to remove excess moisture. Set aside.

2 Combine pepper chunks, onion, carrot and oil in 10-inch nonstick skillet. Cook over medium heat for 4 to 8 minutes, or until vegetables are tender-crisp, stirring frequently.

3 Stir in remaining ingredients, except bulgur. Cook for additional 3½ to 6 minutes, or until mixture is hot and squash is tender-crisp, stirring frequently. Serve over bulgur.

Menu Planning Guide
One serving of this recipe provides:
1 Vegetable
1 Bread, Cereal, Rice & Pasta

Diet Exchanges:
2 starch • 1 vegetable

Hot Pasta Salad

Serve with Spring Lemon Chicken (p 42)
or Turkey Saltimbocca (p 46)

2   *tablespoons balsamic vinegar*

2   *teaspoons olive oil*

⅛   *teaspoon salt*

1   *medium green pepper, cut into ¼-inch*
     strips

½   *medium red onion, cut in half lengthwise*
     and thinly sliced (1 cup)

2   *teaspoons poppy seed*

2   *cups hot cooked linguine (6 oz. uncooked)*

1   *medium tomato, cut into thin wedges*

4 servings

1 Combine vinegar, oil and salt in small
bowl. Set aside.

2 Spray 12-inch nonstick skillet with nonstick vegetable cooking spray. Heat skillet over medium heat. Add pepper, onion
and poppy seed. Cook for 4 to 6 minutes,
or until vegetables are tender, stirring frequently. Reduce heat to medium-low. Add
linguine and tomato. Cook for 1 to 1½
minutes, or until hot, stirring frequently.
Add vinegar mixture. Toss to combine.
Serve hot.

Menu Planning Guide

One serving of this recipe provides:
1 Vegetable
1 Bread, Cereal, Rice & Pasta

Diet Exchanges:

2 starch • 1 vegetable

Jalapeño Curly Noodles

Serve with Fresh Spring Rolls (p 94) or Baked Eggrolls (p 63)

2 tablespoons soy sauce

1 tablespoon sugar

2 teaspoons rice wine vinegar

1 pkg. (5 oz.) Japanese curly noodles (soba),
    broken

2 teaspoons toasted sesame oil

4 oz. fresh shiitake mushrooms, stems
    removed and thinly sliced (1½ cups)

3 cups coarsely chopped bok choy

1 to 2 red and green jalapeño peppers, seeded
    and thinly sliced

2 cloves garlic, minced

1 teaspoon grated fresh gingerroot
    Toasted sesame seed

servings*

*s a main dish, this recipe makes five 1-cup
vings.*

1 Combine soy sauce, sugar and vinegar in 1-cup measure. Set aside. Prepare noodles as directed on package. Rinse and drain. Set aside.

2 Heat oil in 12-inch nonstick skillet over medium heat. Add mushrooms. Cook for 2 to 3 minutes, or until tender, stirring frequently. Stir in bok choy, peppers, garlic and gingerroot. Cook for 3 to 4 minutes, or until bok choy is tender-crisp, stirring frequently.

3 Reduce heat to low. Stir in soy sauce mixture and prepared noodles. Cook for 4 to 6 minutes, or until mixture is hot and flavors are blended, stirring frequently. Garnish with toasted sesame seed.

utrition acts	Amount/serving	%DV*	Amount/serving	%DV*
rving Size /2 cup (111g) rvings er Recipe 10	Total Fat 2g	2%	Total Carbohydrate 13g	4%
	Saturated Fat <1g	1%	Dietary Fiber 2g	7%
alories 76 Calories rom Fat 14	Cholesterol 0mg	0%	Sugars 1g	
	Sodium 249mg	10%	Protein 4g	
	Vitamin A 25% • Vitamin C 25% • Calcium 6% • Iron 6%			
	*Percent Daily Values (DV) are based on a 2000 calorie diet.			

Menu Planning Guide

One serving of this recipe provides:

1 Vegetable
½ Bread, Cereal, Rice & Pasta

Diet Exchanges:

½ starch • 1 vegetable

Mediterranean Pot Stickers

Serve with Vegetable Fried Rice (p 109), Basmati & Wild Rice with Fennel (p 92) or couscous

2 cups cooked lentils

⅓ cup crumbled feta cheese

¼ cup finely chopped onion

1 tablespoon snipped fresh dill weed

1 clove garlic, minced

½ teaspoon grated lemon peel

¼ teaspoon pepper

12 eggroll skins (7-inch square)

2 tablespoons water

2 teaspoons olive oil

¼ cup hot water

6 servings

1 Combine lentils, feta, onion, dill, garlic, peel and pepper in medium mixing bowl. Set filling aside.

2 Cut 6-inch circle from each eggroll skin. (Use inverted 1½-pint mixing bowl as template.) Cover eggroll skins with plastic wrap to prevent drying. Place 2 tablespoons filling on bottom half of 1 circle, ½ inch from edge.

3 Brush edges lightly with water. Fold top half over, pressing with fingers to seal. Bring corners together, overlapping slightly. Brush lightly with water to seal. Keep pot stickers covered. Repeat with remaining filling and eggroll skins.

4 Spray 12-inch nonstick skillet with nonstick vegetable cooking spray. Heat oil in skillet over medium heat. Add pot stickers. Cook for 2 to 3 minutes, or until bottoms of pot stickers are light golden brown. Add hot water. Cover. Reduce heat to medium-low. Simmer for 8 to 10 minutes, or until water boils off and bottoms of pot stickers are golden brown. Serve warm with dollop of plain yogurt, if desired.

Nutrition Facts	Amount/serving	%DV*	Amount/serving	%DV*
Serving Size 2 pot stickers (133g) Servings per Recipe 6 Calories 231 Calories from Fat 47	Total Fat 5g	8%	Total Carbohydrate 35g	12%
	Saturated Fat 3g	13%	Dietary Fiber 5g	20%
	Cholesterol 15mg	5%	Sugars 2g	
	Sodium 353mg	15%	Protein 11g	

Vitamin A 2% • Vitamin C 4% • Calcium 10% • Iron 20%
*Percent Daily Values (DV) are based on a 2000 calorie diet.

Menu Planning Guide

One serving of this recipe provides:

½ Meat, Poultry & Fish
1 Bread, Cereal, Rice & Pasta

Diet Exchanges:

2 starch • ½ fat

Rice with Beans & Jalapeños

Serve with Hickory Beef Fajitas (p 17)
or Chicken-filled Corn Bread Crepes (p 49)

1   *cup water*
1/2 *cup picante sauce*
1/2 *cup sliced green onions*
1 1/2 *cups uncooked instant white rice*
1   *can (16 oz.) pinto beans, rinsed and*
     drained
1   *tablespoon canned diced jalapeño peppers*
1/2 *teaspoon ground cumin (optional)*
1   *medium tomato, cut into wedges*

6 servings

1 Combine water, picante sauce and onions in 2-quart saucepan. Bring to boil over high heat.

2 Stir in rice, beans, peppers and cumin. Cover. Remove from heat. Let stand for 10 minutes.

3 Before serving, fluff rice with fork. Garnish with tomato wedges.

Nutrition Facts	Amount/serving	%DV*	Amount/serving	%DV*
Serving Size approximately 1 cup (237g)	Total Fat <1g	1%	Total Carbohydrate 38g	13%
	Saturated Fat <1g	1%	Dietary Fiber 7g	28%
Servings per Recipe 6	Cholesterol <1mg	0%	Sugars 3g	
Calories 188 Calories from Fat 7	Sodium 136mg	6%	Protein 8g	

Vitamin A 4% • Vitamin C 15% • Calcium 6% • Iron 15%
*Percent Daily Values (DV) are based on a 2000 calorie diet.

Menu Planning Guide
One serving of this recipe provides:
1 Bread, Cereal, Rice & Pasta

Diet Exchanges:
2½ starch

Spanish Rice

Serve with Hickory Beef Fajitas (p 17)
or Chicken-filled Corn Bread Crepes (p 49)

1   *teaspoon vegetable oil*

1   *small onion, chopped (1/2 cup)*

2   *cloves garlic, minced*

2   *cups water*

1   *can (14 1/2 oz.) stewed tomatoes, undrained*

1   *cup uncooked long-grain white rice*

1   *medium green pepper, chopped (1 cup)*

2   *teaspoons chili powder*

1   *teaspoon instant beef bouillon granules*

1/2 *teaspoon dried oregano leaves*

1/2 *teaspoon pepper*

2   *tablespoons snipped fresh cilantro leaves*
      or Italian parsley

10 servings

1 Heat oil in 12-inch nonstick skillet over medium-high heat. Add onion and garl Cook for 3 to 5 minutes, or until onion is tender-crisp, stirring frequently. Stir in remaining ingredients, except cilantro.

2 Bring mixture to boil. Cover. Reduce heat to low. Simmer for 17 to 20 minute or until rice is tender and liquid is absorbe stirring occasionally. Remove from heat. S in cilantro.

Nutrition Facts	Amount/serving	%DV*	Amount/serving	%DV*
Serving Size 1/2 cup (127g)	Total Fat 1g	1%	Total Carbohydrate 22g	7%
Servings per Recipe 10	Saturated Fat 0g	0%	Dietary Fiber 2g	6%
Calories 105	Cholesterol 0mg	0%	Sugars 3g	
Calories from Fat 10	Sodium 204mg	8%	Protein 2g	

Vitamin A 10% • Vitamin C 25% • Calcium 2% • Iron 8%
*Percent Daily Values (DV) are based on a 2000 calorie diet.

Menu Planning Guide
One serving of this recipe provides:
1/2 Vegetable
1   Bread, Cereal, Rice & Pasta

Diet Exchanges:
1 starch • 1/2 vegetable

Vegetable Fried Rice

Serve with Mediterranean Pot Stickers (p 103), Spicy Chicken Wontons (p 40) or grilled chicken breast

Sauce:

/4 *cup frozen cholesterol-free egg product, defrosted; or 1 egg, beaten*

2 *tablespoons rice wine vinegar*

2 *tablespoons low-sodium soy sauce*

/2 *teaspoon ground ginger*

/8 *teaspoon pepper*

1 *teaspoon peanut oil*

1 *cup sliced fresh mushrooms*

/4 *cup chopped red onion*

/2 *cup diagonally sliced green onions (1/2-inch slices)*

1 *medium carrot, shredded (1/2 cup)*

/2 *cups cooked long-grain white rice, chilled*

servings

1 Combine sauce ingredients in 1-cup measure. Set aside. In wok or 10-inch nonstick skillet, heat oil over high heat. Add mushrooms, onions and carrot. Cook for 1 to 1½ minutes, or until red onion is tender-crisp, stirring constantly. Stir in rice.

2 Pour sauce over rice mixture. Cook for 1½ to 2 minutes, or until rice is hot and sauce is thickened, stirring constantly.

Nutrition Facts	Amount/serving	%DV*	Amount/serving	%DV*
Serving Size /3 cup (131g)	Total Fat 1g	1%	Total Carbohydrate 21g	7%
servings Per Recipe 6	Saturated Fat 1g	1%	Dietary Fiber 1g	5%
Calories 112	Cholesterol 0mg	0%	Sugars 3g	
Calories from Fat 9	Sodium 221mg	9%	Protein 4g	
	Vitamin A 53% • Vitamin C 8% • Calcium 3% • Iron 8%			
	*Percent Daily Values (DV) are based on a 2000 calorie diet.			

Menu Planning Guide

One serving of this recipe provides:
1½ Bread, Cereal, Rice & Pasta

Diet Exchanges:

1½ starch

Index

Cy DeCosse Incorporated offers
a variety of how-to books.
For information write:
    Cy DeCosse Subscriber Books
    5900 Green Oak Drive
    Minnetonka, MN 55343